# ENGLISH

## An outline for
## the intending student

# Contributors

Angus Ross
G. K. Hunter
D. J. Palmer
Gabriel Josipovici
R. B. Le Page
Gerald Moore
Andrew Hook
Laurence Lerner

**Edited by Angus Ross**

# ENGLISH

## An outline for the intending student

Routledge & Kegan Paul   London

First published 1971
by Routledge & Kegan Paul Ltd
Broadway House, 68–74 Carter Lane
London EC4V 5EL
Printed in Great Britain by
C. Tinling & Co. Ltd, London and Prescot
© Routledge & Kegan Paul 1971
ISBN 0 7100 7138 8 (c)
ISBN 0 7100 7139 6 (p)

# Contents

# Preface

The purpose of this book is to inform students who intend to
read English at the British universities of the kind of choices
available to them, either of institution or of kind of course.
Students may also read for degrees in English at some other
institutions of Higher Education, such as Polytechnics and
Colleges of Technology, but the scope of this volume excludes
any discussion of this set of choices. The *Sunday Times* newspaper carries at certain times of the year lists of courses,
including English, which are available in non-university
institutions.

In an Introductory essay, I have tried to set out the nature of
some of the choices of course available, and why courses take
the form that they do, as well as to direct attention to the real
difference between kinds of courses rather than the superficial
marks such as the different texts which are read. From experience in university admissions I am only too well aware on
what uninformed and superficial grounds serious decisions are
often made. The Appendices give a minimum of information to
base choice on, and suggest where more information may
be found.

The body of the volume consists of seven essays covering
different kinds of English studies. This rather clumsy descriptive title has been preserved to indicate that English literature
may be only part of such a study, though it may be the dominant part in most cases. Professor Hunter discusses the discipline of literary criticism, that kind of study which places
literary discrimination at the heart of the matter. Mr D. J.
Palmer presents the argument for the historical study of English

literature, a mode of study which has in the past formed the basis for university courses in English literature not because other organizational principles had not been thought of, but because it represents a fundamental principle of the subject matter itself. Mr Gabriel Josipovici outlines the kind of consideration which lies behind the organization of English study as part of a study of European literature. This has been a possible choice for many years either in general degrees or in joint honours degrees, where the student could combine an English course with a course in French, German or some other language. Quite what *context* this places his English study in was often vague, and as Mr Josipovici shows the introduction of modern, imaginative works into the curriculum has placed this kind of approach in a new light. Professor Le Page gives an account of the potentialities of the study of the English language as part of English Studies, potentialities which transcend in significant and exciting ways the old, rather narrow, historicist philology, though that study too has still its importance as it always had its rationale. Mr Gerald Moore and Dr Andrew Hook introduce the possibilities of studying literature which is not written in England, or even Britain. The corpus of American literature is already extensive and impressive and its nature raises important intellectual and imaginative problems. Non-western English literature, too, forms an exciting study which places the British student's own cultural environment in a profoundly different light, a desirable slant for study. Lastly, Professor Lerner chooses the connection which may be made between literature and psychology as an illustration of a kind of study which is becoming both more important and increasingly available as a choice to the student. This particular combination of interests is probably only possible for graduate students who have already mastered some body of reading and discussion, but similar juxtapositions of diverse disciplines are increasingly common in university courses.

No attempt has been made to be exhaustive in the choice of essay topics, but rather the intention is to show the variety of possibilities, as well as the rationale of different kinds of study, old as well as new. It ought to be emphasized that the best way of looking at new developments in the subject is that they permit many different kinds of study. They do not replace traditional modes of discussion which are founded on rational and coherent principles that, however, may not be to the taste of all. Although it is thought and argument which must prompt choice, this volume does not take any theological position in the disputes about the 'true' kind of study of English literature, just as it does not argue that the study of English literature is the central or most important part of university study in general. Plenty of persuasive advice is available from eloquent advocates of one or other of the competing philosophies, and the Bibliography contains the titles of books and essays for further consideration.

A.R.

# Acknowledgments

I should like to thank my fellow contributors who produced their essays promptly and with entire good will to this project. I should also like to apologize for the delay in organizing their contributions into a volume, which was caused by the editor's struggles with the complexity of the Appendices. The information in the Appendices was produced by patient colleagues in the different institutions and the descriptions of each university's English courses is also based on invaluable information from the same sources. Profound thanks are due to my informants, the more so since there was no space to give the often extensive descriptions they wrote of their courses and they probably will not in all cases agree with the Editor's summary judgment.

A.R.

The editor and publishers would like to express their thanks for permission to reproduce the following:
Extract from 'Crusoe's Journal' from *The Castaway* by Derek Walcott, Jonathan Cape Ltd.
'A Dream' (Twelve Songs IV) from *Collected Shorter Poems 1927–1957* by W. H. Auden, reprinted by permission of Faber & Faber Ltd.
Extract (edited) from 'Caliban 3' from *Islands* by Edward Brathwaite, Oxford University Press.

# 1

# Introduction: English Studies in British Universities

*Angus Ross*

At the outset, it is necessary to mention two important current developments in British university education. The first of these is the way in which the study of English literature for various reasons has become a kind of general educating discipline, much as the study of the classics was a century ago, or the study of logic was in the late middle ages. The second is the great expansion in the number of students who *apply for* admission to university courses, and the smaller but still great increase in the numbers of students who actually enter them. For both these reasons, a good many young people elect to study 'English' without the kind of vocational or professional motivation that might make a student take up engineering, theology, medicine, Chinese, or biochemistry. They are also making this choice in highly competitive circumstances. There is at the same time, much public discussion of the *rôle* of the universities in our society. Whether they stand outside the political arguments of the times and protect or encourage disinterested investigation, or whether, expensive as they are, they have a clear, even a mass, educational function. Some of the arguments which go on about the *nature* of English courses, the extent of the discipline, the contents of the syllabus, are really arguments about the function of universities, about how many students should be in universities, and about whether the present changes taking place on the educational scene are good or bad. Some of the arguments are simply about money or resources.

Does 'more mean worse', as Kingsley Amis thought of the growth in the number of students, especially English students? Should a greater number of minds be introduced to thought and judgment at a university level, at the expense of destroying the unity of a like-minded, intellectual *élite*? This is not to say that no real intellectual or philosophical arguments exist about the kinds of English courses at the universities, or about their content and their educational or cultural purpose.

Compared with the study of the Greek and Roman classics, of history, or even of modern languages, the study of English literature is a comparative newcomer in the family of university 'disciplines' or 'subjects'. The subject has always been somewhat ill-defined, spreading into contiguous areas of moral philosophy, history, social studies, philosophy itself, or psychology. This is partly because, though English literature was not always formally 'studied', it was always read, and itself formed to some degree the traditions of other studies. Gibbon, for example, is a superb dramatic or tragic narrator as well as a historian. T. S. Eliot has claims to distinction in kinds of thought other than poetry. Also, the early teachers of the subject were themselves students and practitioners of other disciplines, often philosophy, the classics, or history, before they turned to 'English'. It is therefore difficult to talk about the 'traditional' English course. Some, if not most, references to this mythological entity are ritual gestures, like throwing salt over your shoulder, intended to exorcize the demons of change.

One way to view the study of English literature is to conceive of a body of slowly accumulating 'classical' texts, to which the judgment, imagination and sensibility of the student is exposed. In this way, proved, generous and humanizing values are transmitted from the past to the present and into the future. A celebrated statement of this case is F. R. Leavis's argument in *English Literature in our Time and the University*:

> in a lecture on Lord Snow's *The Two Cultures*, [he writes] I myself said, having made some immediately relevant points about the way in which a poem exists for discussion: 'Here we have a diagram of that collaborative process by which the poem comes to be established as something "out there", of common access in what in some sense is a public world. It

gives us, too, the nature of the existence of English literature, a living whole that can have its life only in the living present, in the creative exposure of individuals, who collaboratively renew and perpetuate what they participate in – a cultural community or consciousness. More, it gives us the nature in general of what I have called "the third realm", to which all that makes us human belongs' (pp. 171–2).

Dr Leavis goes on to say that in the 'unprecedented conditions of technological civilization', literary study in the university forms a bulwark against the imposition of values and ends by the non-human, or perhaps anti-human processes of technological development and administrative convenience. I have quoted Dr Leavis in this connection, because he is the most persuasive and influential proponent of what I am suggesting is one of the basic attitudes to English studies. The implication of this view is neatly set out by Professor W. W. Robson in his 1965 F. R. Leavis Lecture, *English as a University Subject*, when he says

the propositions that English literature is a genuine body of knowledge, and that the appropriate discipline for its study is literary criticism, seem to me coupled and to move together (p. 24).

Dr Leavis himself says 'literary study' but in fact in British universities, it is the study of *English* literature that forms the focus of this argument, and the intending student who wishes to read 'English' is at the centre of conflicting pressures.

If the discipline of 'English' centres in the practice of literary criticism, as Professor Robson holds, and that 'literary criticism' is of the particular and special kind that Dr Leavis advocates, then the practitioners of such a hard art will probably be comparatively few. They will be, as Dr Leavis says, 'proper university material'. 'No one should be admitted to read English at any university,' he says in another essay, 'who isn't of university quality and hasn't a positive bent for literary study.' The purpose of the English 'school' in this picture is

to counter the frightening development of our civilisation to which at an earlier stage, Arnold tried to alert his countrymen. It is to replace the educated public, now decayed, that

Arnold after all could count on for audience – replace it by creating a new educated public, and being in relation to it a centre of concentration and a maintainer of standards.[1]

This, it is suggested, is what is meant to take the study of literature seriously.

An opposite view of the university, and hence of the 'place' of English studies in it has been exemplified in Lord Annan's reply[2] to Dr Leavis's argument:

> Dr. Leavis adheres to a belief which I reject. He believes that there is one set of values and one set of ends which all men of good will who desire to live 'creatively' would agree upon and define in the same terms. I don't. I believe in the morality of pluralism . . . there are many good ends . . .

Earlier in the same piece he wrote, 'Universities should hold up for admiration the intellectual life. The most precious gift they have to offer is to live and work among books or in the laboratories.' Obviously this view is not incompatible with the maintenance of a small intellectual *élite* as one of the aims of the university, but equally it doesn't imply it, and Lord Annan is in fact operating an expansionist argument in his essay.

The implication of the latter picture for English studies is to make that area, like other humanities subjects, more inchoate, less well defined. 'English literature' tends to be everything written in the language which can be studied in a number of different ways, with the practitioners of Dr Leavis's critical art (or at least those holding his doctrines) forming only one of several groups which might be made up of historians, linguists, bibliographers, philosophers, social scientists, all deeply interested in literature, and all endeavouring to exercise to some degree critical sensibility.

From the point of view of Dr Leavis and like-minded thinkers, Lord Annan and academics of his persuasion are branded with the masks of 'blankness', 'sciolism [pretentious superficiality of knowledge] and bogus intellectuality'. To the other side, Dr Leavis and his followers may seem like a crowd of turbulent cobblers shouting 'there's nothing like leather'. The provincialities of British academic life, however, are to some degree obscuring an intellectual division in the study of literature which is deep enough, and old enough. On the one hand, we may ask if literature *can* form the material for study of different kinds and risk being relegated to the background as a suspect discipline, perhaps at best the 'cultured' recreation of those engaged in some 'real' discipline? Or, on the other hand, is the study of literature, perhaps for us especially English literature, something of supreme importance which involves 'preserving, while it is still a living continuity, the only [culture] we have – to keep it alive and in growth . . .'?[3]

Mr Josipovici's essay in this volume places the question of the nature of tradition in a wider historical and European context, and he shows also that the development of 'modernism' in literature has raised fresh complexities in the argument. Dr Leavis doesn't really deal with those complexities, since Eliot and Lawrence are as yet the *terminals* of his historical argument. Mr Moore's essay gives some idea of the difficulties which may rise in thinking of 'our culture' in literary terms, and Professor Le Page's essay shows that other kinds of investigation which are legitimately involved in 'English Studies' may make quite impressive and general claims of their own.

Divisions of opinion such as those between Dr Leavis and Lord Annan, or indeed between Aristotle and Plato, about the nature of the literary art and the aims of education are reflected in the syllabuses of English courses in British universities. By this I don't mean lists of prescribed texts, but whether there is a 'body of knowledge' to be studied that may be designated 'English literature 1360–1560', or 'Tragedy', and what might the difference be between two such entities. Since universities are up to a point democratic institutions, it is most unlikely that single-minded programmes like Dr Leavis's will become dominant. Pluralist views which admit of compromise or if not compromise at least mutual toleration, will be most likely to prevail. Universities shelter some men who think quite hard about what they are doing, not a comfortable occupation. Such men will sometimes seek to change established arrangements, but at the same time universities are complex institutions and as such possess in some measure that inertia which makes corporate thought slow to change, and slow to take form in action. The pluralist, intellectualist view of the university is in the present context the older. In fact, Dr Leavis's kind of view is a reaction against it. The syllabuses of English programmes, therefore, are often largely historical, fragmented, with components that are meant to demand a number of different skills, including it may be said the kind of collaborative criticism of which Dr Leavis is a distinguished practitioner. For example, a syllabus may well contain courses which set out to study a genre like the novel, as if the genres were like the 'families' of plants, as well as courses in which the social context of writing is considered in such a way as would philosophically preclude holding notions of 'developing' genres. The rationale of this philosophical inconsistency is to expose the student to different kinds or categories of thought and judgment.

This pluralism is further emphasized by the arrangements found in many universities in which joint honours courses are possibilities. In such courses, a student may spend half his time studying English literature, and the other half practising, or familiarizing himself with some other discipline such as history or music, or the study of a foreign language and its literature. The same pluralism is probably at the root of the General Degree courses to be found here and there, in which 'English' is only one of the subjects to be studied. The old requirement of making some study of Anglo-Saxon and Middle English compulsory is also a vestige of similar attitudes, not only, as might be thought, to make the soft option of reading fiction and poetry stiffer. The requirement showed an almost instinctive belief that the study of one's native literature had other intellectual and historical implications. The requirement is still found, based on cogent arguments, but these have now broadened into more general linguistic considerations, or into the field of the comparative study of cultures.

Another kind of English course has developed in recent years. This develops the notion that some fruitful contact may be made between different disciplines, and is to be found exemplified in the 'integrated' English courses to be found at some of the new universities. Such courses are meant to require the study of English literature or the practice of literary criticism in a context of other disciplines or other cultures. They seem to be what Dr Leavis dismissively calls 'cosmopolitan cures for our provinciality'. Cosmopolitan, either by introducing the student to American, African, Asian or general European culture, or by introducing him to other disciplines. In this volume, Mr Josipovici, Dr Hook and Mr Moore all, in different ways, discuss the former possibility, and Professor Lerner examines the latter. There is nothing absolutely new in this, as a study of older General Degree and Joint Honours syllabuses, will show. Single Honours courses often require the study of subjects outside English or literature. Indeed any good student would not normally pass his time at a university without encountering these possibilities. What *is* new, is the degree to which such contextual work is now being organized, and brought into conscious discussion.

It is more than likely that a good number of students will have some idea of the kind of interest they have in English literature, since their teachers will have taken some position or other in the conflicts I have discussed, and will either have inspired or antagonized their students accordingly. I am concerned here to point out that such positions are taken on reasoned grounds and are not a matter of whim. Neither, since they have profound personal, philosophical and practical implications, are they unimportant.

In deciding what courses seem best suited to his or her needs, a student should keep one or two points in mind. If a camel is a horse designed by a committee, an English course is probably a blue-print for study designed by a university committee. New ideas in arranging courses do not necessarily *replace* old ones, they offer more and different kinds of choices. Every kind of university course has a rationale. It is up to the student to decide, if he can, how that rationale fits in with his own ideas. Or, perhaps better, how his ideas connect with the rationale, because the theories of literature come only after a great deal of reading. It saves a good deal of time to have a dogma that tells you Sir Walter Scott is not a good novelist because he was a lawyer. Any argument about the romantics, however, eventually involves Scott's fiction and it is impossible to discuss it without reading it. A prospective student should discuss the principles of different courses, so far as they may be apparent, with the best informed professionals he knows, his English teachers. It is idle to choose a course because the books mentioned, if some titles appear here and there, *look* interesting. All courses allow the students to read. It is the *kinds* of study that are important, the aims of the course. For example, a course might be meant, in a historical framework, to provide the student at the end of his university career with a wide and fairly comprehensive knowledge of what has been written in English between certain dates. This is no useless possession. On the other hand, a positive requirement to study Anglo-Saxon or some sociological topic will be found peculiarly difficult by different people. The expectations of what the course will accomplish in the personal life and insights of the student may be pitched very high and be disappointed, especially if an apocalyptic view is held of literary study. English courses are taught by people with widely varying conceptions of what they are doing. This disunity is, to my mind, stimulating; it is also sometimes for the student frustrating. It is, however, produced not by ill-will but by the variety of human nature, which is also a quality reflected in literature itself.

## Notes

1. F. R. Leavis, 'English Unrest and Continuity', lecture published in *The Times Literary Supplement*, no. 3509, 29 May 1969.
2. Lord Annan, 'The University and the Intellect', *The Times Literary Supplement*, no. 3557, 30 April 1970, 465–6.
3. F. R. Leavis, *English Literature in our Time and the University*, Chatto & Windus, 1969, 182.

# 2

# The Discipline of Literary Criticism

*G. K. Hunter*

People go to university to read English for a mixture of motives, and many of these must, in the current situation, lead to disappointment. It is often thought that 'English', not tied to the drudgery of facts, and acknowledging the importance of personal response, will in some undefined way liberate the individual from submersion in 'the way things are', at home, in school, in company. The pupil hopes he will find a way of expressing his personal valuations so that they become generally accepted. The study of literature can only do any such thing in fact if the energy for liberation is the pupil's own energy. Literary study, or the teaching of literature (the usual precondition), can only provide a discipline, a containing focus within which the energy of the questioning individual can be concentrated, being directed to material that can be dwelt with or returned to again and again. In the course of this 'discipline' new and coherent views can emerge. But these views (of life or society) are mere by-products; they are not part of the discipline. Literature is not life, nor can it stand-in for it. The study of literature is not the study of life; the experience of life is not a qualification for success; all has to be submitted to the procedures and practices that are relevant to a rational and self-consistent pursuit. The claim that literary criticism stands at the centre of university study will not be made in this essay. Its concern is with what university English has in fact within its current capacity, leaving remote consequences and pious hopes for other apologies.

If the immediate function of an English course in a university is (as I suppose) to enable more people to read and hear better the variety of effects available in their mother tongue, then the function of the present essay should be to suggest some ways in which better reading and hearing can be encouraged and worse reading and hearing revealed for what it is – and the basic word for this is, I think, 'unsustaining'. I should make the point as early as possible that I believe it is the literary teacher's business to be concerned with the bad reading of good literature, but not with bad literature itself ('good' and 'bad' in this sentence meaning whatever the teacher thinks of as good and bad). I assume that the badness of bad literature is not a proper object for direct attack, inside a teaching situation – but I shall return to this point later in the essay. The mode of communication that is proper to literary teaching relates to a shared or imputed enthusiasm for the good book; but the opposite may be implied by the nature of our description of what we admire. Good reading (the capacity which stands at the centre of all English courses at present available) is a skill which can be sustained and in its turn sustains further reading. It can be sustained because it brings a large number of books (and experiences of life) into such a manifold relationship that they continue to be observed not only without decay of attention but with constantly changing and even developing insights and interests. This implies a continuous sense of purposiveness in reading, and a continuous enriching of one reading in terms of another.

I assume that good reading is best sustained by a method of study which applies to a large number of books and which supports the transition from one book to another. Such a framework will inevitably imply certain exclusions, certain preferences. I do not think it inevitably follows that the framework which excludes or depresses fewest areas of potential literary experience is the best. On the other hand preferences so keen and exclusive that we have to enjoy very little and to be sustained less by purposive enjoyment than by moral superiority are probably suspect. It seems clear that before one can enjoy any one thing with understanding one must have enjoyed many others, for good or even bad reasons. The problem of 'depth' versus 'breadth' is one that frustrates all those who have to devise literary courses. The two virtues can hardly be inculcated simultaneously; but one without the other leaves the student only half prepared for criticism. Those who devote their time to reading few texts with great care (as in much A-level teaching) must be without sufficient sense of what kind of work they are dealing with, for they are without experience of the range of alternatives open to the author or of the range of responses possible for the critic. On the other hand those who read many texts, at the speed necessary to cover a sufficient range, run into the danger of not understanding any of their texts properly. They may, of course, be on the road to understanding; but the time-scale of a degree-course is not likely to be sufficient to allow them to reach the goal. Any system of education is likely to do violence to what may be thought of as the natural pace of learning. This problem is inherent in all systems of learning involving more than one person.

One of the ways in which the literary student will be expected to hold in a sustained attention the various kinds of reading he undertakes will be by means of a critical outlook which aims at coherence. It is obviously important to avoid the slow decay of impression which is the fate of even an excited reading of a book in the minds of most readers. This is obviously a problem for students in all book-based subjects; but the answer for literary reading must be different from that appropriate to other subjects. In most cases it is necessary to remember, in as systematic a manner as possible, what the author said; for the literary reader it is the quality of the book and of the experience that must be retained and tied in with such system as can be made relevant. It is often said that the crucial reading of an important book is a permanent modification of our consciousness. The discipline of literary criticism is ideally concerned with charting and interrelating such modifications and noting the recurrence of effects from book to book; it is the practical business of a literary course to pursue the books we read in such a way that we encourage the effort towards a comprehensive unity. Students of politics or philosophy who read courses in English often find its 'discipline' evasive and unsatisfactory. They expect their knowledge of Milton to be parallel to their knowledge of Hobbes or Marx – usually an abstract summary of the man's whole position, together with some detail of particular arguments. But in English we read *Comus* or *Paradise Lost* for their unabstractable qualities, for some coherent sense of the things actually 'there', and for the systems of meaning we can establish between ourselves and the external existence of our texts.

The ordering of literary relationship between ourselves reading and the books we read (which we call criticism) is as resistant to abstraction as is the literary experience itself. It is sometimes supposed that the coherence of criticism depends on a characteristic vocabulary and that this can be reduced to order by abstraction; that 'the theory of literary criticism' or 'the history of literary criticism' provide ordered areas of teaching and learning free from dependence on personal experience. The error here seems parallel to that which supposes that 'the history of science' is a substitute for the actual experience of scientific investigation. In neither case does a mastery of the vocabulary lead to a mastery of the subject. 'The theory of literary criticism' seems to derive its coherence from philosophy; 'the history of literary criticism' when it is not a test of memory – 'What was Burke's position on the Sublime?', 'What do you remember of Horace's remarks about imitation?' – is usually a branch of intellectual history. In neither case are the disciplined procedures being followed attached directly to the central experience of reading. It does not in fact seem possible to treat criticism as a separable part of literary teaching; it is rather the mode by which a continuous commerce with literature sustains itself. Without the backing of personal experience, insight decays into cliché, integrity into smartness, criticism into journalism.

Since critical power is inseparable from personal experience it is natural to raise the question, 'Can it be taught?' One must admit that in the strictest sense it cannot. A man whose ear is deaf to all the tones of literature cannot be caused to hear. But most ears can be trained, that is, encouraged to discover a more discriminating response to a wider and wider range of literary experience, so that small but vital clues will be noticed, leading to perceiving how this poem or novel can be read, so that relevant questions can be asked. In this process it is important to start where the reader *is*, so that the individual's complicity in the expansion of reading can be preserved. One of the recurrent problems in the discipline of literary criticism is posed by the tendency to prefer vocabulary to experience, to prefer the glamour of criticism to the glamour of literature. Many people come to university in good command of the gestures of criticism, but with only imperfect knowledge of few books. In order to recover integrity of response they may have to seem to go backward to simpler and more obvious observations which are in fact within their possession. Even then there will probably remain a considerable difficulty in distinguishing actual observation based on the text from ideas which originated somewhere else. It is one of the stranger paradoxes about university 'English' that it is commonly agreed that literary criticism involves a creative process of discovery by the individual student, and that the only valid preparation for it is an increasing familiarity with the text; while at the same time literary criticism continues to burgeon and provide short-cuts to understanding or at least to successful essays. Is it fair to demand (as most tutors do) that the student prefer a re-reading of the text to a reading of the critics? What if the first response to the text is a blank? May it not follow that the second reading will repeat the blank? Would it not be more appropriate to find out how *anybody* could feel enthusiasm for the work in question? The very first sight of an appropriate attitude may bridge the gap between the pupil and the text and release a whole stream of personal and relevant comment. Or it may spark off so thorough a rejection of these critical attitudes that the alternatives emerge unbidden. The relevant factor here, which would seem to defend the inclusion of some criticism among the student's reading, is the speed with which the critic can be superseded, his attitudes absorbed into the genuinely personal reactions of the student, and attention returned to the text which will validate or devalue all remarks about it.

It is sometimes supposed that the reading of a plurality of critics releases one from excessive dependence on individual critics. The production of 'Casebooks', where ninety per cent of the reading-matter may be critical rather than literary, seems to mean however that the principal effect is the disappearance of the text beneath the welter of critical controversy. The questions that appear at the end of these volumes are most often of the kind: 'Distinguish between the attitudes of Professor A and Professor B.' This is certainly easier than the formulation of a personal attitude, but it is also less worth while; for it does not grow, as part of our personal experience, to form our future sensibility.

In reading a critical essay, then, a tutor is looking above all for a fresh and even vivid sense of the works under discussion, seen from as comprehensive and coherent a point of view as possible. He is looking above all for a developed sense of relevance. The student must learn to know what thoughts are relevant to the work being discussed, and at what point their relevance ends. It is only through a sense of relevance that information can be turned into judgment. An important difference between English and other academic subjects is that the student ought to be able to surprise his tutor with new and true insights. Major works are, to all intents and purposes, inexhaustible; the complexity of their organization allows their coherence to be glimpsed from an almost infinite variety of viewpoints. It will be strange if the tutor cannot suggest a more effective organization of insights; but insight itself – a new relevance in quotation, a surprising new collocation of figures and ideas – is available to anyone who keeps his eye on the literary fact. The merely factual is, of course, insufficient. Essays which simply 'tell the story' or 'describe the plot' are at a stage of formation which is preliminary to actual criticism. Expertise will often show by a capacity to co-operate with the reader's assumed knowledge of the book, taking giant steps through its more obvious elements, but never deserting the sense of its continuity.

'Knack' or 'flair' are as useful here as in other pursuits. The gift for a turn of phrase may betray its possessor; but the effort to convey how it feels to be in contact with *King Lear*, or to yield to a sudden glimpse of what *Clarissa* is about, requires a fair amount of literary skill. In such cases of course, it is difficult to separate the capacity to write from the capacity to see: to know it is to know how to say it.

The subjectivity, which is an essential and I believe inescapable part of any discipline within which we try to hold together our literary experience, is often thought of as a disabling factor. But it is also a peculiar strength. English is a subject which every Englishman believes he knows about. Its students are constantly required to defend what they are doing, not only against charges that the subject is 'useless' (not of immediate practical utility) but also that it is incapable of discipline, being at the mercy of whims and tastes. It is fortunate that the questions are usually fired this way round; for the student of literature ought, by the nature of his subject, to be capable of giving answers to these comments. Probably only he in the university has the opportunity to create out of his personal experience a discipline – that is, a consistent and coherent body of priorities and assumptions – which grows by taking in new material and modifies both itself and the material by the processes of digestion. The strength of such a discipline is shown by the speed and accuracy with which it can attach the new and genuine to the old and tested, deploying hypotheses and forecasts on the good basis of a coherent and wide-ranging but always personal sensibility.

What is often meant by the complaints against English is that the lower levels of 'discipline' are hardly catered for. There is very little of central importance that can be learned by heart. This absence of rote-learning is often disturbing to the student. In many subjects much of the undergraduate's time must be spent in trying to acquire the language in which his personal capacity for creative originality (if he achieves it) must be phrased. In English the problem is different. The mother tongue is the language of our native capacity to respond. We have to learn to straighten the channels of our creativeness, not dig the first sod. In the absence of tables of facts, however, the English student's knowledge sometimes seems invisible to him. His skills do not exist except in the context of his reading. None the less he has these skills; and in some ways they resemble those that appear in mathematics or philosophy. In these subjects (and no doubt others) the student learns to recognize the paradigm behind the example. When he is faced by a new problem his first move is to reduce it to its simplest form and then apply the rules. This is parallel in a very rough way to the skill of the critic. He has read many books and has gradually acquired a sense of what may be generally appropriate to this book or to that. He learns not to read novels as if they were essays, or lyrics as if they were satires; he learns to discriminate between periods and between genres, to adjust speeds of reading and organize his expectations of 'what will happen next'. But the paradigm and example model of learning will not take us very far into criticism. There the reduction to a simplest form will always involve falsification; the work, if it is good, must retain at all times its capacity to surprise. There is no such thing as 'the answer' to a critical problem; skill at reading a poem only means effective co-operation with it, not possession of it.

In saying this I may be running counter to the claims of F. R. Leavis whose notion of the 'possession' of a poem often seems to imply that there is one 'right' reading of every work. He says that

> Analysis . . . is the process by which we seek to attain a complete reading of the poem – a reading that approaches as nearly as possible to the perfect reading (*Education and the University*, p. 70).

Leavis's notion of 'the perfect reading' ignores the extent to which criticism belongs to rhetoric rather than dialectic. It is perfectly possible for criticism to be 'true' without any claim that it is 'the truth' about a poem. The best criticism ever written – say the comments of Dr Johnson or Coleridge on Shakespeare – leaves the work, like the reader, unexhausted; our capacity to respond anew has been augmented rather than depressed. Criticism is in this respect rather like a series of two-dimensional reports of a three-dimensional object – topographical line-drawings of a mountain for example. These will differ greatly from one another, and it will always be possible for a new artist with a new technique, with the sun or moon at a different point, or standing at a different angle, to offer a different but 'true' description of the mountain. With our knowledge of the actual mountain we may accept or reject the drawings as more, or less, representative. The word 'irresponsible' is certainly within our power and may properly be applied to the draughtsman who has failed to make anything relevant to the object itself. At the level of the student essay it is appropriate to mark down the signs of bias, of axe-grinding, of self-absorption, of a failure to understand the meaning of the word at the time the poem was written, misinterpretation of rhythm, an ignorance of relevant allusion. But what might seem at first sight to represent ignorance and irresponsibility can subsequently be proved to be part of a coherent interpretation which meshes, in its turn, into a larger system of values and assumptions. When the tutor says, 'The poem builds up in this way, doesn't it?' the pupil is perfectly right (though not usually able) to say, 'No, it builds up in this quite different way.' In the end such disputes are about whole systems of thought or ways of life, and may lead only to the mutually exclusive dogmatisms of taste or to an agreement to differ. What the educational process should concern itself with is not the answer but the method by which any mode of answering would have to move if it were to be valid. This does not mean, however, that criticism must confine itself to the appreciative or (at best) the inflammatory. It may belong to the realm of rhetoric, but this still requires it to be concerned (like legal rhetoric) with the analysis of facts; 'irrelevance' and 'irresponsibility' are still appropriate dismissals.

One of the problems that will recur in the conversations of those who seek to defend criticism against the charge that it is only an elaboration of the obvious, concerns the relation of form and content. The 'undisciplined' reader is liable to suppose that books are to be valued for what they say in a more or less explicit manner, and to talk about the content on the assumption that he is talking about the book. 'Style' is often thought of in these terms as 'good writing', and 'good writing' is conceived of as conformity to some ideal standard of English prose laid up in an unchanging heaven under the special guardianship of H. W. Fowler. To discover that style and content are two sides of the same coin, that synonyms do not exist in literature, that the way of speaking alters the nature of the thing said – this is to learn that conventional discourse about books is less rich and all-involving than need be. The exploration of works of literature is the exploration of the human mind, not only the conscious and controlled part, that part concerned with civilized discourse – where the form/content distinction may seem possible – but the solitary panic of the unconscious and half-understood as well. The appropriate languages of literature range from the supercilious to the fragmentary; and the critic must be willing to engage with all of these; it may be his business to bring back rational descriptions of quite irrational experience. The notion that the critic should use impressionistic criticism to convey impressionistic literature is erroneous. Criticism is in the first place directed to the formulating intellect; the openness of its mode to objection and counter-objection, appeal to evidence, citing of authority, requires a set of rational rules by which its rhetorical business can be regulated. It is only by accepting the limitations of such a rational discipline that we can discover the full function of criticism to make a bridge between the rational world and irrational experience, not only confirming but also enlarging the scope of our sympathetic experience.

Another fallacy that the critic must avoid derives from the same wish to stay inside the fold of the explicit and the conscious. The painful indefiniteness of self-scrutiny can be evaded, it is often assumed, if we know what the author intended. Alas, this is another short-cut leading into the wilderness. Few authors seem to operate in terms of an *intention* that can be defined better outside than inside their creative work. Many writers speak of the work 'growing under their hand', of 'the characters taking charge', of 'being forced into an ending they did not anticipate'. John Livingstone Lowes's description of the creative processes behind Coleridge's *Ancient Mariner* and *Kubla Khan* indicates the extent to which an author may draw on associative patterns that cannot be supposed ever to have been part of his conscious mind. Authors, when questioned, are usually evasive about the meaning of work they have written; sometimes they give meanings which contradict one another. Clearly their statements have a particular authority; but it is not an absolute authority. The critic is free to describe his experience of the book in ways which contradict the statements of the author, and we may properly prefer the critic's description to the author's. He is also free to use terminology which may have been unknown or even abhorrent to the author. It is entirely proper (if unhelpful) to describe Hamlet's dilemma in relation to the Oedipus complex, provided that we do not then proceed to blame Shakespeare for failing to give a full account of the Oedipus complex. It is not at all improper to describe *Wuthering Heights* in terms of the Marxist analysis of nineteenth-century society. The description of the art object takes place today in a mind which is acquainted with the concepts of Marx and Freud, and is designed to affect other minds similarly equipped. If these ideas are useful means of focusing and projecting what the critic sees in the work, the ignorance of the author is irrelevant.

A distinction is often made between 'criticism' and 'scholarship'; embattled positions are taken up on an assumption that these two are mutually exclusive competitors for the student's attention, acceptance or practice of one implying hostility or contempt for the other. Nothing could be more mistaken. Scholarship is a necessary preliminary to most good criticism. Accurate and thorough knowledge of the author's text, his manuscripts, his revisions, his sources, of his language and even of his life, can be avoided only by those with a strong taste for resounding error. Pursuit of these things does not by itself lead to criticism; but the immediate critical response which is not tested against them is likely to prove hollow.

One must allow that criticism and scholarship belong together and not in opposition. None the less one can see how they have come to be regarded as polar opposites. They represent what might be described as the conservative and radical approaches to literature. They are linked in this with a further distinction – between an emphasis on the literature of the past on the one hand, and on the other an emphasis on the literature of the present. It might indeed seem to some that the process of judging the literature of the past is not at all in the province of criticism, but in that of literary history – another part of the island, another chapter of the present book. But these divisions are wholly arbitrary, and in this case it would be distorting to think of them as more than temporary conveniences. The recovery of the 'meaning' of works of the past is, it is true, tied in with the whole process of understanding the past; to revalue the society which produced (say) Shakespeare's plays is in some measure to revalue the plays it supported. Certainly we have to learn by error and patient attention that the past is different from the present in nuance no less than in grand design. But this is only one side of the critical coin; we have also, before we can deal with the literature of the past, to bring the invisible assumptions of our modern being into an objective focus. The judgment on past literature, no less than present, derives from the current stance of the judging mind. It is obvious that the criticism of past literature is 'safer', less adventurous than criticism of our contemporaries. Time has winnowed the wheat from the chaff, and the relative value of this and that is fairly stable. But the notion that literary history deals with authors who, being dead, are fixed, can only derive from the most flaccid view of historical scholarship. The relationship between works written in the past and readers living in the present must always be a dialectical one. Our literary entrée into the past enables us to see the current scheme of values from a point outside the present; but the position 'outside' can only be created in relation to the present, for it is made up by a selection of those elements from the past that seem significant to the critical attention of the present. The criticism of literature exists between the polarities of mere taste and mere fact, of purely subjective response and purely objective existence; but at neither pole is there more than a sterile purity.

Though criticism of past literature and criticism of present are always together *between* the poles of subject and object, they are likely to be given different emphases. The urgency that many feel in their response to contemporary literature makes it difficult to keep a sense of the work 'out there', unpossessed by our responses, however violent. On the other hand the range of subjective responses is likely to become more limited as we move backward in time.

Those courses which stop the study of literature at some safe date (1880, 1914 or 1939) obviously suppose that discipline and excitement do not belong together. Presumably they feel that after some such date the tutor will no longer be able to 'give the answer'. But in what important sense can the tutor give the answer about Milton or Wordsworth? He can point to things that have often been thought (this usually means in the period 1820–1940) – that Satan is the 'hero' of *Paradise Lost*, or that the Falstaff of *The Merry Wives of Windsor* is a poor shadow of the character of the same name in *Henry IV* – but unless the tutor can derive these views from his own personal stance he will not be able to use them effectively. As I have said above, in criticism the right answer may be less important than the right method, a method which allows for the conversion of personal impression into self-consistent argument. A whole degree-course devoted to modern literature might be excessively subjective. If we consolidate our personal feelings by testing them against more impersonal criteria – the tradition within which the author is writing, the relation of this work to his whole *oeuvre*, the generic assumptions of his form – we may think that in modern literature the testing mechanism is insufficient. The tradition in which the author works is also the tradition inside which we ourselves think. This remains true even when the work is part of that *avant-garde* designed to vex and disturb the settled mind. Our 'hatred' of such work seals in fact our immediate relationship to it. Who bothers to feel hatred for the *avant-garde* of the past? Modern work operates essentially *inside* our responses; hence its power to irritate, and hence also the difficulty of testing our personal responses against it. The mode of modern writing is so much the mode of our own expression that we are likely to see only the subject matter and to develop our responses only into arguments with the author: 'I would not have put it that way', 'he has misrepresented the truth', 'how unbearably poignant is his expression of *my* situation!' On the other hand, a course devoted exclusively to the past is in danger of discounting or discouraging personal response. The student is unlikely to feel free to be bored by *King Lear* or to despise both Donne and Milton; the weight of allegedly objective evidence on the other side seems too great to be lifted into balance. But for all the difficulties, it seems to be true that the life of past literature must stand in the mind of the critical present. On the other hand a truly critical interest in contemporary literature can hardly be sustained except in the perspectives supplied by our knowledge of the past.

The mode of literary teaching which begins with scholarly information and then goes on to critical judgment is common and perhaps inevitable. But it has great disadvantages. It is hard to give scholarly information without prejudging critical response. If a class is told that the second quarto of *Hamlet* is probably printed from Shakespeare's manuscript and that the Folio text derives from a theatrical prompt-book it may well be difficult or impossible for them to respond to the Folio cuts as improvements (as, in some senses, they are). But the alternative is unpractical. To begin in natural ignorance and relive the history of civilization, stumbling forward from the revelation of one error to the shuddering impact of another – this would be an ideal education, but only for Methuselahs. Inside a normal time-scale some measure of direction and prejudgment is inevitable; the danger of rows of identical pupils intoning identical second-hand opinions cannot be wholly avoided.

One mode of teaching literature is often thought of as avoiding the scholarly and other prejudging preliminaries which impede direct confrontation between the reader and the work of literature – the method of presenting the pupil with passages typed on a blank sheet of paper and asking for comments based on reading thus, without the prejudgments of date and authorship. This 'practical criticism' has obvious advantages. It places upon our reading, squarely and excruciatingly, the burden of understanding what is being said, and how these words manage to say it. The reader is brought up against his own unexamined assumptions, his powerfully distorting prejudices, his self-protective blindness. All literature, it might be thought, is reduced to the condition of contemporary literature. There is, however, one important respect in which this is not true: the passage on the sheet of paper may be without context for the pupil, but it is not so for the tutor. The notion of a known and confirmed truth, settling the question once and for all, is not in fact taken out of the system; it is only concealed in the operation of it. For this reason the inductive method of practical criticism is liable to be thought of as a game, guessing at answers which are known to be right or wrong by the application of quite different criteria. Nor does the exercise seem particularly appropriate to those without a fairly extensive knowledge of literary history. The 'placing' of an unknown poem is largely a matter of thinking what other poems are like it; if we have not already in our minds, labelled and pigeon-holed, a series of examples or specimens it will be very difficult for us to classify the new poem and to discover the appropriate way of reading it.

From all this it would appear that practical criticism is liable to be a way of concealing scholarship rather than dispensing with it. It may, of course, still be a convenient method of acting out the process of discovering the evidence which is relevant. I must confess myself extremely doubtful about the common process of putting two poems side by side, one 'good' and one 'bad' and then encouraging the student to discover which is which. There is a danger here (as in all small-group teaching) of substituting brain-washing for education. The student is 'free' to discover for himself the evidence which will support an inexplicit but pervasive view of life; he is much less free to find valid evidence tending in the opposite direction. Most learn very quickly, from a mixture of motives, not all of which are bad, the vocabulary of the tutor's party line. This almost certainly includes a statement that these views are derived directly from unmediated contact with literature.

Another argument against the general validity of practical criticism derives from its difficulty in dealing with certain kinds of literature. The method is specially appropriate to the lyric poem; longer poems are harder to handle. They tend to be built up on general ideas which cannot be understood inductively. *Paradise Lost* cannot be read properly if we have no knowledge of Christianity, of the epic tradition, of Milton's life and times. The system of using 'representative passages' may be effective; but the criteria by which 'representativeness' is decided are not themselves found by practical criticism; and these criteria determine in advance what it is appropriate for the reading of each passage to discover. Further, it is more difficult to handle prose than verse; the novel is resistant to the method; for the novel depends on the reader's continuous process of responding. This is inevitably falsified if we stop for the close analysis of samples. It is like stopping the car engine to see how it is working. Even in the chosen plot of lyric poetry there are problems. Certain kinds of lyric are more suitable for treatment: poems marked by complex structure, by irony, density of metaphor, dramatic or quasi-dramatic flashes of brilliance are especially welcome – the poetry of Donne and Herbert, Shakespeare's Sonnets, and some eighteenth-century verse. Other good lyrics – Blake at his most transparent ('Infant Joy' for example), or Wordsworth's Lucy poems – yield less to what T. S. Eliot has called the 'lemon-squeezer' school of criticism. It is not improper to note the difference between Donne and Wordsworth; but if we believe in practical criticism as an effective method it is hard not to take the next step and assume that the difference is one of value. Some kinds of poetic virtue have come to seem more central than others simply because this method of approach gives them particular prominence.

The limited approval of practical criticism that I have argued for above implies that it is a useful means of revealing rhetorical virtues in poems we already know or believe to be good. Its great merit is that in its discussion of these virtues it keeps us close to the poem itself. The interrelation of buried rhetorical detail and a felt enthusiasm for the whole poem gives the process of exposition a close and apposite logic. This logic cannot, however, be transferred to poems for which we do not feel enthusiasm. It sometimes seems to be assumed that the system can simply be stood on its head: if certain devices are found in good poems then their opposites will be found in bad poems; all we need to do is point to these bad devices ('loose' rhythm, 'cheap' personification, 'trite' imagery, etc.) and then the badness of the poem in question will be proved. We are not, however, in literary criticism dealing with a world of simple opposites. The good poem affects us by giving us possession, however temporarily, of a world at once luminous and coherent; it is possible for us to describe this and communicate our sense of how it is. The opposite is not a corresponding set of negative qualities. It is usually a simple failure on the author's part to make any effect on us at all. To try to deal with bad (that is, unsuccessful) poems by the inductive methods of practical criticism is to push its processes into regions where they do not work. To start from the nothing we feel to be on the printed page, and try to build on that, is to go nowhere. Of course it is perfectly possible to speak illuminatingly about failures if we have a clear sense of the poetic norms by which good poetry will always succeed. Thus Dr Johnson in his *Lives of the Poets* can speak with perhaps even more memorable effect about failures than about successes. When he tells us that Pope's *Dunciad* has as its chief fault 'the grossness of the images . . . ideas physically impure such as every tongue utters with unwillingness and of which every ear shrinks from the mention', he relies on general assumptions about taste and propriety, which every man is expected to share. But the practical critic is seeking to avoid these prior assumptions. I suspect he does so, when he deals with poems he does not admire, only by hiding them. Behind the talk of deficient rhetoric ('loaded with abstractions', 'using a literary vocabulary', etc.) lie more basic assumptions about 'bad' social attitudes – assumptions necessarily pernicious because concealed and likely to be banal if they have to be concealed.

It is true that literature is, in some sense, the product of society, and that it expresses, in some sense, the nature of the society in which the author lived. It follows that criticism of literature involves criticism of society. But the process by which literary criticism is transformed into social criticism must be of labyrinthine complexity. It is in the superficies of his manners that a man is 'average' or 'representative' and these are not the aspects of a man with which the profound statements of art are concerned. The effectiveness or radiance of a Millamant (in Congreve's *The Way of the World*) does not depend on her existence as a lady of the Restoration period. It derives from her (or Congreve's) capacity to use the manners of her social group as adjuncts of humanity, and so to make a claim on our modern human response, through them. Our capacity to feel our modern selves into the world of Restoration high life, through our identification with Millamant, may lead us to be aware of elements in that life that we cannot accept. But our assent to Millamant should keep us from a simple supposition that the art of this brutal and licentious society must be brutal and licentious. The notion that we can tell the health of a society (whatever that means) by taking the pulse of its literary productions is very suspect. I believe that in such investigations the literary evidence is commonly used to bolster judgments already made on other grounds. I think most people would allow the truth of this, as it applies to the past. But there is a variant form of the argument which, when applied to the modern world, commands wide assent. Many people seem to believe that the study of English will enable them to discriminate between the 'genuine' and the 'false' throughout contemporary culture. 'Culture' in this sense is not, of course, the best that has been thought and said, but (more anthropologically) the means by which groups express their relationship with their environment. The decline of formal commitment to religious explanations of man's estate has meant that literary models of behaviour have been increasingly scrutinized to provide answers to the question, 'How should we live then?' Many people begin to study English believing that it will supply answers to this question. And mentors are not lacking to assert or imply that its function and its importance are attached to its capacity to make sense of the contemporary world.

I do not wish to deny that the reading of novels and poems may have a genuinely liberating effect on human sympathies. We find ourselves identifying with minds and experiences quite different from our own; and in this sense literature enables us to understand more of the world in which we live. But this effect of reading (not necessarily critical reading) is very different from that which is sometimes assumed – that we learn by reading critically to reject undesirable aspects of our society. There is little doubt that the methods which can be used to discuss the virtues of Donne and Herbert, Hopkins and Eliot show a blank when applied to the jingles of the ad-man or the lyrics of the Beatles. But this makes little more than the obvious point that these modern cultural expressions are embedded in a different social setting. It does not tell us that the social setting is corrupt or corrupting. The idea that those who can enjoy Donne and Hopkins must dislike pop-music and television and Blackpool and all objects made of plastic involves a conjunction no more necessary than the one which it outmoded – that the capacity to construe Greek prose conferred an expertise in governing the outposts of the Empire. There is no evidence that the study of literature makes us better at anything other than the study of literature. But if we have achieved this we have achieved much. To those who can accept the limitations of its discipline the sustained and sustaining pursuit of literature is a permanent enrichment of their capacity for experience and of their ability to be, not moral, not 'right', but human.

# 3

---

# The Historical Study
# of English Literature

*D. J. Palmer*

Literature, Aristotle said, is more philosophical than history; literature deals with universals, while history is concerned with particulars. History is the study of the past; yet what Ben Jonson wrote of Shakespeare is surely true of all literature that is worth studying: it is 'not of an age, but for all time'. Is the historical study of literature therefore a contradiction in terms?

In one sense, certainly, literature has no history, since it is not something which happened. A literary work is not itself an event, although its composition, its publication or performance, and its reception by readers are all events that may be established and studied by the historian, as he may analyse and describe the conditions in which it was produced, biographical, social, and intellectual. A writer's choice of a particular form, of a particular source or model, and of particular words may also be regarded as historical actions which in themselves and their attendant circumstances are the historian's concern. Almost all of the facts about literature, indeed, are historical facts; the identity of the author, the date of composition, even the authenticity of the text as it was written, are only the most fundamental of these facts. Literary history is therefore concerned with facts about literature; but since most (though admittedly not all) histories of literature are not simply encyclopedias, the literary historian, like other kinds of historian, is interested in relationships of cause and effect between these facts, and in questions of continuity and development. Students of Shakespeare, for instance (to illustrate the discussion throughout the chapter from the figure we have already taken as representative), have recently been told that not only did the use of the Blackfriars theatre by the acting company to which Shakespeare belonged immediately precede his writing of the last plays, but that this event actually accounts for certain characteristic features of these plays. Here we have an example of the attempt to relate two kinds of evidence, the historical and the literary, for an analysis of the features of the plays concerned has to be made in literary terms. Both sets of evidence may be accurately defined, but the link between them is a matter of historical judgment rather than fact. The very conception of Shakespeare's last plays as a homogeneous group depends upon their shared characteristics as revealed by literary comparison and analysis, as well as upon the historical evidence of their common authorship and chronology. And these questions of dating and authorship, where historical evidence is lacking, may have to admit the literary testimony of form and style. As literary history is more than a collection of unrelated facts about literature, therefore, the problems with which it is concerned are historical in character, but the methods it employs are both literary and historical. There is no simple antithesis between literary history as 'objective' fact and literary criticism as 'subjective' judgment. Literary history cannot determine literary values, yet neither can it ignore them.

Literary values seem least relevant when the historian is using literature to document social history or the history of ideas. Shakespeare's plays, for instance, may reflect contemporary attitudes to love and marriage, social order, patriotism, and justice, subjects of interest to the historian, while their dramatic and poetic excellence is a matter of indifference to him. Indeed, since the question is one of representativeness, an inferior writer may serve this kind of historical purpose better, and often does. Nevertheless the use of the subject-matter of literature as historical evidence always has its dangers, for there is a tendency to confuse literary convention with social behaviour. There is no reason to suppose, for instance, that young ladies of Shakespeare's time were addicted to disguising themselves as boys, although this is what frequently happens in Shakespeare's comedies, and not in his alone. If this is thought an unlikely error for even an historian to make, it is the same kind of reasoning which lies behind the familiar argument that the popularity of revenge tragedies among the Elizabethans reflects a prevalent anxiety about the ethics of revenge in contemporary life. The historian who wishes to refer literature to contemporary life is on safer ground when he turns his attention from plot to literary form. Methods of literary construction, of presenting reality and ordering experience, will reveal more than the taste of contemporary readers; from a comparative study of different authors in this way there can emerge important evidence about the basic mental habits and assumptions of an age – evidence, moreover, for which there are few alternative sources. Thus, in Elizabethan literature the characteristic emblematic imagery and the use of structural analogies and parallelism (for instance, in narrative technique and dramatic sub-plots) provide their own testimony to a world of established relationships and values such as the historian of Elizabethan society or thought is concerned with. But since the analysis of literary form is not in itself an historical task, the historical purpose in this case too depends upon literary method.

The distinction between ends and means has enabled us so far to regard literary history and the study of literature-as-history as two independent and perfectly legitimate undertakings employing literary methods for historical purposes. By the same token the critical study of literature does not lose its autonomy when historical methods and historical evidence are introduced. If there is a theory of literary studies, a definition of their claim to an identity of their own, then clearly this must be based upon literary values. It is therefore true that the essential discipline of literary studies is the discipline of literary criticism. But in describing literary criticism we are acknowledging that it shares in common with other disciplines a concern with the relevance and validity of the evidence upon which its judgments are based. 'Comparison and analysis are the tools of the critic,' wrote T. S. Eliot, adding, 'You must know what to compare and what to analyse.' It is in this respect that historical considerations make their claim upon the critic's attention.

A classic statement of the case for historical criticism is that made by Dr Johnson in his *Proposals for Printing the Dramatick Works of William Shakespeare* (1756):

> When a writer outlives his contemporaries, and remains almost the only unforgotten name of a distant time, he is necessarily obscure. Every age has its modes of speech, and its cast of thought; which, though easily explained when there are many books to be compared with each other, become sometimes unintelligible and always difficult, when there are no parallel passages that may conduce to their illustration. Shakespeare is the first considerable author of sublime or familiar dialogue in our language. Of the books which he read, and from which he formed his style, some perhaps have perished and the rest are neglected. His imitations are therefore unnoted, his allusions are undiscovered, and many beauties, both of pleasantry and greatness, are lost with the objects to which they were united, as figures vanish when the canvas has decayed.

The argument has become a familiar one. A writer expresses himself in terms of the 'modes of speech' and 'cast of thought' of his age; when these are obsolete, the writer is 'sometimes unintelligible and always difficult', and 'many beauties . . . are lost'. Historical insight is therefore necessary to recover a proper understanding and estimation of the literature written in the past, otherwise criticism cannot function accurately or adequately. However it is admittedly difficult to understand how a writer can 'outlive his contemporaries' to become the subject of critical admiration in later times, if he also becomes 'necessarily obscure', his greatness dimmed by the passage of time. Is the permanence of great literature dependent upon the criticism that operates in an historical perspective? How is the relevance of historical evidence to be determined? In the remainder of this chapter we shall consider the claims made for this kind of historical study of literature.

There is a story about an experiment to determine the original language of man. One version of it relates that King James VI of Scotland placed an infant boy in the foster-care of two deaf mutes on the Bass Rock, an otherwise uninhabited island, and when he visited the island several years later, he found to his great satisfaction that the boy was speaking perfect Hebrew.

The situation of the literary critic is similar to that of the Scottish king; his is not a genuinely empirical study, because he brings to his subject a complex set of assumptions and associations. Some of these he may erect into deliberate principles and standards of judgment, but some inevitably remain as hidden presuppositions. Even the most elementary understanding of literature requires some previous experience of life and language, so that the critic's preconceived ideas and expectations are in the first place the necessary means by which he can come to terms with a literary work. Literary values, like King James's linguistic theory, appeal to abiding and universal truths, independent of time or place; literary judgments, on the other hand, involve processes rather like those which led the king to recognize what he heard as Hebrew.

Even when some of the assumptions and presuppositions on which criticism is based are demonstrably false, however, the consequence is not necessarily bad criticism. Critical approaches to Shakespeare from a generation after his death until recent times tended to assume that he was an ill-educated writer, whose achievements were those of sheer native genius, the triumphs of an untutored creative instinct. The critical evidence of the plays themselves, which were 'irregular' in construction according to classical (and therefore, it was thought, to universal) standards, was supported by the testimony of Shakespeare's own contemporary, Ben Jonson, who in the same verses that proclaimed Shakespeare 'not of an age, but for all time', had referred explicitly to his 'small Latine, and lesse Greeke'. Yet however wrong-headed neo-classical criticism was about Shakespeare's faults, it was certainly not blind to his greatness, and Dr Johnson was not the only eighteenth-century critic of Shakespeare with questionable assumptions but penetrating insights. The attitude to Shakespeare as 'nature's poet' persisted through the Romantic period, itself a great age of Shakespeare criticism, and through most of the nineteenth century, until some students of Shakespeare were unable to reconcile the historical evidence of cultivated tastes which they found in the plays with the preconceived notion of their author as a rustic genius innocent of book-learning, and therefore concluded that the plays were not written by Shakespeare at all. The Baconian controversy, and others like it, belong to the lunatic fringes of literary history rather than to criticism, but the fact remains that the assumptions which were thus brought to the surface and exposed had long underlain critical interpretation and evaluation of the plays. These assumptions were about certain historical issues: the significance of Ben Jonson's observation on Shakespeare's learning, the ignorance of historical evidence about the arts of poetry and drama as Shakespeare and his contemporaries understood them, the ignorance of the traditions in which Shakespeare was writing. They did not on this account always produce bad criticism of Shakespeare, but they certainly controlled the kinds of critical approach that were made.

Thus by virtue of being unhistorical, criticism may nevertheless be making certain historical assumptions. Another kind of disguised preconception which is common enough in criticism concerns its attitude to literary development, whether in the case of the individual author or in that of a genre. Criticism is too often inclined to treat what historical evidence shows to be early work with a patronizing or even a dismissive air. This is quite apparent in prevailing critical attitudes to Shakespeare's earlier plays, for instance, where terms such as 'immature', 'experimental', 'apprentice work' are frequently encountered, implying that the chief critical interest of these plays lies in their anticipation of things to come. The critic's assumption here is that we should not expect too much from early work, and this lowering of expectations often has led to an undervaluation of work concerned. In such cases, criticism not only relies upon the historical evidence of chronology, but presupposes gratuitously that literature obeys the laws of organic development or of evolution from primitive beginnings to maturity, and this in itself is a false kind of historicism.

Although the history of criticism is more than the history of taste (there are permanent values to which criticism makes appeal), many of the concealed assumptions and preconceived ideas which inevitably underlie critical approaches to literature are historically determined. It is a commonplace that each age reinterprets for itself the literature of the past; critical judgments are provisional, but they are not invalid for that reason. What Dr Johnson said of literature is therefore also true of criticism: 'every age has its modes of speech, and its cast of thought'. The Augustan approach to Shakespeare was obviously very different from that of the Romantics; Bradley's interpretation of the tragedies could only have been conceived in the later nineteenth century, as Wilson Knight's studies reflect the working of a twentieth-century mind. Nevertheless there is a fundamental difference between a recognition that our own age sees Shakespeare in terms of contemporary critical presuppositions and the proposition that Shakespeare can be considered as a twentieth-century writer. Many critics have approached the plays without much understanding of their historical context, but few have felt the need to bring them up to date and place them in a specifically modern context. This however is the avowed principle of interpretations such as those of Jan Kott in *Shakespeare Our Contemporary*: 'not of *his* age, but for *our* time'. Kott reads Shakespeare in the light of the modern experience of totalitarianism, revolution, the concentration camps, Freud, and existentialism: not surprisingly, the Shakespeare that emerges bears a curious resemblance to Samuel Beckett, Jean Genet, and other dignitaries of the Theatre of the Absurd. What one objects to in this interpretative method are not so much the distortions, as the diminishing effect. Where other criticism, of whatever period, has addressed itself to the Shakespeare whose qualities are for all time and therefore of greatest value, the Shakespeare of Jan Kott is by definition a more limited, impoverished figure, with scarcely any recognizable identity of his own. Moreover, even on his own terms Kott's modern version of Shakespeare rests upon a conception of the contemporary world that is partial, narrow, and remarkably unsubtle.

While criticism is therefore bound in some degree to reflect the values and prejudices of its time, the example of Kott suggests that critical interests are not served by making a virtue of this necessity. But the function of historical criticism is not merely to exchange the values and prejudices of one age for those of another. By extending the critical context, by introducing us to other possible ways of considering a literary text, historicism can greatly enhance and refine our critical awareness, and lead us to examine more carefully the assumptions and attitudes we bring to bear upon our reading. The justification of referring literature to its historical context is that it improves our understanding of those qualities which are 'not of an age, but for all time'.

Historical criticism interprets and evaluates literature in the light of historical evidence. It reverses the ends and means of literary history; as literary history may use critical methods to determine matters of historical interest, historical criticism assesses the evidence of literary history to establish matters of critical interest. By no means all the evidence of literary history is of equal value or relevance to historical criticism, but we can never be sure that any piece of evidence is altogether without critical relevance. T. S. Eliot wrote, 'Any book, any essay, any note in *Notes and Queries*, which produces a fact even of the lowest order about a work of art is a better piece of work than nine-tenths of the most pretentious critical journalism, in journals or in books.' It is true that good critics are even rarer than good poets, but the critic and the historian are not in competition with each other; indeed, the good literary scholar has to be both.

'When a writer outlives his contemporaries . . . he is necessarily obscure': as Dr Johnson's words imply, the method of historical criticism is one of reconstruction. Its aim is to recover what has been lost or forgotten, not out of antiquarian curiosity, but to put us more completely in possession of the literature we are studying. The obscurities which it sets out to illuminate are of two kinds: those which the uninformed modern reader recognizes, and those of which he is not even aware. Thus, in the language of a given text, some words may be strange because they have become obsolete, and some are still in usage but may have changed their meaning. In the first case, we know that we need the help of historical evidence, but in the second case we are likely to be unwittingly misled unless our approach to the work as a whole is historical. Hamlet's soliloquy, 'To be or not to be', for instance, contains the words 'quietus' and 'fardels', which are unfamiliar because we do not meet them in modern English, and the meaning of 'coil' in the expression 'this mortal coil' is only partially found in the modern sense of the word, but what is to warn us that 'undiscover'd' means 'unrevealed' not 'unknown', or that the perfectly familiar modern word 'conscience', so crucial to this speech and to the play as a whole, has more than its perfectly familiar modern connotations?

What is true of individual words applies also to considerations of style. Dr Johnson found something absurd about Lady Macbeth's line, 'Nor heaven peep through the blanket of the dark': 'I can scarce check my risibility, when the expression forces itself upon my mind,' he wrote, 'for who, without some relaxation of his gravity, can hear of the avengers of guilt *peeping through a blanket*?' To his critical judgment, the image seemed lacking in the dignity he thought appropriate to tragedy. But how far is this suggestion of a timorous figure cowering beneath the bedclothes a distraction, brought about by accidents of historical change in the overtones of the word 'peep', which then in turn control the connotations of 'blanket'? If historical evidence shows that, at the time when *Macbeth* was written, 'peep' was as free as 'look' from low associations, then the image that provoked Dr Johnson's amusement was largely of his own making. Modern readers have a similarly comic distraction in Gertrude's description of Hamlet in the duel as 'fat, and scant of breath', a phrase that, despite one suggestion that it alludes to the ageing Burbage who created the part, actually refers to the sweat of vigorous exertion, not the effects of superfluous weight. If, on the other hand, the historical evidence supports Johnson's reading of Lady Macbeth's line, then his sense of its incongruity reflects a neo-classical conception of decorum which obscures from him the effectiveness of the image. For it not only hints at the actual circumstances of the murder she is planning, but in addition suggests the frailty and defencelessness of the forces of good, in keeping with many other passages in the play.

The modern reader is not likely to share the critical prejudices of the eighteenth century, but there are other instances in which he is prone to a lack of imaginative sympathy. For example, the long speech on the Salic Law given by the Archbishop of Canterbury at the beginning of *Henry V* is something very like a touchstone of modern embarrassment over matters of rhetorical propriety in the plays. When the speech is taken at its face value, criticism tends to be severe and the speech is often omitted from performance; apparently it can only be accepted today either as a comic turn (this was how it was presented in the Olivier film), or as a piece of Machiavellian irony. The speech is not to be judged purely on its style, of course, but an important element in modern attitudes to it is our distrust of rhetorical persuasion. The same suspicion of eloquence is surely also manifested in T. S. Eliot's celebrated refusal to accept Othello's last speech, which he denounces sternly as 'bovaryism'. Many of the witty exchanges of word-play in the comedies are similarly found tiresome to modern taste. The least that historical criticism can do in such cases is to show that the loss is ours, and to demonstrate that the style of the plays is governed by a decorum, even if it does not correspond to our own. At least we can avoid the otherwise arrogant assumption that ours is the only possible response to such matters.

Questions of style are closely related to the other formal conventions governing the structure, characterization, and mode of presentation in any literary work, just as literary form itself is the expression of ideas and attitudes that are moral, social, or metaphysical in nature. Here the kinds of obscurity that concern the modern reader are less likely to be those that he finds inexplicable than those of which he may be unaware. Quite unhistorical assumptions will usually allow us to find the plot and characters of a novel or play intelligible: the problem of obvious obscurity through historical ignorance, as in the case of unidentifiable words, does not arise so frequently when we are analysing character-motivation or the moral import of a work. This is particularly so in the study of English literature, since the continuity of our cultural tradition means that shifts of moral and social attitudes have taken place in a com-paratively narrow compass, compared, for instance, with the kind of adjustments we should have to make if we were study-ing Oriental literature. Experience of examining overseas students of English literature, to take a parallel situation, certainly suggests that when the cultural tradition is less familiar, even the simplest elements of plot and character can sometimes either prove incomprehensible or undergo weird transformation. One therefore suspects that in a subtler if a less colourful way, our confidently unhistorical interpretations are often prone to miss the point, or to blur the issue. The

awkward problem of the relation between art and reality underlies most considerations of form and meaning: thus, for
instance, generations of critics believed that Shakespeare's
comedies were carelessly constructed because their plots are
so full of improbabilities and illogicalities. For many, indeed,
this was their special virtue as pure make-believe entertainment
without any serious reflection upon life. While criticism does
not need historical evidence before challenging this point of
view, the chances of unaided critical effort inferring from the
plays alone the nature of such conventions as pastoralism,
Petrarchism, and Ovidian metamorphosis are about as remote
as those of the proverbial twenty-thousand monkeys who,
according to statistical probability, might one day produce
Shakespeare's text on their typewriters. Shakespeare's comedies
are illuminated by a knowledge of the conventions, because
much of their artifice and sophistication exists in their use of
the conventions as a point of reference: the joke is lost when
it is not understood. In the notorious final scene of *The Two
Gentlemen of Verona*, for instance, the romantic hero volun-
tarily surrenders the girl he loves to the friend who has betrayed
him, a gesture which must seem absurd and meaningless until
it is regarded in the light of the conventions of courtly romance,
and then it is just absurd but not meaningless. The figure of
Shylock presents similar problems to the modern reader, whose
repugnance at the idea of anti-semitism may well dominate his
feeling towards the character, and consequently determine his
attitude to the whole play. Interpreted historically, Shylock is
certainly a much subtler character than the conventional stage-
Jew, but that convention is a better frame of reference in which
to consider him.

Since historical criticism is concerned to restore not merely
what has become absolutely unintelligible, but the lost meanings that remain otherwise undetected, its approach must be to
the work as a whole. And above all, the important question it
asks is 'What is the meaning and value of this work?', not
'What did this work mean to its author, or to the age in which
it was written?' The meanings that existed in the mind of the
author, or in those of contemporary readers, are simply beyond
recovery, apart from the objection that in any case these are
not the legitimate subjects of critical interest. Neither does the

D

historical approach allow us to read a text as though we were contemporaries of its author: the aim is not so limited, nor so impossible. The end of historical criticism, like that of other kinds of criticism, is to enable us to see the work for what it is; but it is not a form of super-criticism that can offer an infallible, definitive, and 'objective' account of literature.

Historical evidence is a guide, not a key, to interpretation and evaluation; indeed, historical information only becomes evidence when we can show its relevance to a critical understanding of literature. The historical context is therefore something we create, our frame of reference, which obviously can only be partial and fragmentary in relation to the theoretically infinite context of total history, partly because we select what we consider appropriate, and partly because there are limits to our knowledge. Otherwise all historical critics would arrive at identical conclusions, which demonstrably and fortunately they do not. We may choose to place the text we are studying in relation to the author's personal or professional circumstances, in relation to other works by the same author, in relation to works of a similar kind by contemporaries of the author, in relation to the prevailing critical theories or beliefs of the age in which it was written, and so on; the context may be narrow or extensive, simple or complex. In historical criticism there is no such thing as the 'complete' context, any more than there is a 'complete' meaning of a work of literature.

The chief weakness to which historical criticism is prone is not its inability to define the total context, but its tendency towards abstraction in moving from the particular to the general. Thus convenience of reference, and little else, has determined the conception of the literary period as a self-contained historical unit; we all know that English literature is divisible into so many periods, like the strata which the geologist identifies in a rock-face, but not as clearly defined. Provided these periodic divisions are recognized as purely arbitrary ways of slicing up the cake of English literature for easier handling, they are harmless enough. Works written in chronological proximity, like works written by the same author, do share a family resemblance while preserving their own identity. A writer's language, his attitudes and assumptions, the formal structure of his work, will all be illuminated by comparison with the usage of his contemporaries, but this historical evidence is only a point of departure for understanding his work; the family resemblance should not be used as a kind of lowest common denominator for interpretation. In generalizing about a period, particularly when we turn from the literature itself to the wider horizons of its social and intellectual life, the danger is that of creating an historical context on the basis of hypothetical norms, and then of interpreting literature as the expression of these norms. A literary work is always more than merely representative, and less than wholly typical, of its period, and works of major importance in particular cannot be reduced to the standards of the average or the commonplace. In this respect we must be careful how we use the evidence of popular attitudes, conventional ideas, and prevailing orthodoxies in the interpretation of literature. Otherwise the historical context becomes a straitjacket, forcing works of rich imaginative life into a narrow and falsifying conformity. A sensitive understanding of a period sees it not as a static, uniform, and self-contained entity, but as a dynamic and diversified phase of history, containing both progressive and conservative forces; in this sense, all periods are ages of transition. Moreover such an understanding will realize that works of literature are not merely passive reflections of the historical forces determining the character of their age, not merely to be seen as expressions of an abstracted 'background', but as active agents of the processes of continuity and movement in their time.

The way in which we see the past must be that of our own time; our sense of history is a modern sense. History, like literature, is constantly subject to reinterpretation and reassessment: there is no last word on the subject, although we sometimes deliver our pronouncements as if the occasion were the Day of Judgment. Paradoxically, therefore, historical criticism offers what are essentially modern interpretations of literature. The meanings recovered by its methods are those that are meaningful to our minds, though, as with good criticism of any kind, not necessarily to our minds alone. But a work of historical criticism belongs to its age as much as the criticism of Johnson and Coleridge belongs to theirs: it could not have been written at any other time. The historical sense itself makes us recognize this. Nevertheless the claim of historicism is not that its interpretations are made *sub specie aeternitatis*, but that it keeps the present in touch with the past. Every age has its own kinds of ignorance, and therefore something to learn from the past: this is not why we read literature, but it is a good reason for learning to read it historically.

It seems appropriate at this stage to demonstrate how these general principles and considerations might be borne out in practice. What follows is therefore not a full historical interpretation of *Hamlet*, but an outline of particular problems in the play as they might be approached historically.

As we have seen, there is an obvious necessity for historical evidence in the case of unintelligible language. This is the problem of meaning in its most elementary form, and *Hamlet* has at least its fair share of problems of this kind. Not all unfamiliar words are unintelligible: the meaning of many, if not of most, can be reconstructed from the context. And the cause of obscurity is not always archaic usage: such features of the author's style as metaphor, paradox, and ellipsis may make the language difficult, without being unintelligible to the perceptive reader or listener. But when we encounter words that utterly baffle comprehension, words that we simply do not recognize, we usually need recourse to some kind of historical evidence.

Take for instance these lines from Hamlet's speech in Act One, Scene Three, immediately before the entry of the Ghost:

> This heavy-headed revel east and west
> Makes us traduc'd and tax'd of other nations;
> They clepe us drunkards, and with swinish phrase
> Soil our addition; and, indeed, it takes
> From our achievements, though perform'd at height,
> The pith and marrow of our attribute.
> So, oft it chances in particular men
> That, for some vicious mole of nature in them,
> As in their birth, wherein they are not guilty,
> Since nature cannot choose his origin;
> By the o'ergrowth of some complexion,
> Oft breaking down the pales and forts of reason;

Or by some habit that too much o'erleavens
The form of plausive manners – that these men,
Carrying, I say, the stamp of one defect,
Being nature's livery or fortune's star,
His virtues else, be they as pure as grace,
As infinite as man may undergo,
Shall in the general censure take corruption
From that particular fault. The dram of eale
Doth all the noble substance of a doubt
To his own scandal.

The general drift of the speech is probably comprehensible to most modern readers, but we are capable of only a blurred understanding unless words and phrases such as 'traduc'd and tax'd', 'clepe', 'soil our addition', 'vicious mole of nature', 'pales and forts of reason', and 'plausive' are within our grasp. The glossary will help here, but as always it can only give a rough and ready assistance by offering modern approximations to the meaning of obsolete words. When we come to the final sentence of the speech, however, the glossary is of no help. There are two obvious problems in this sentence: the word 'eale' and the grammatical structure. In the context of 'dram', we might guess that 'eale' has something to do with 'ale', assuming that 'dram' is the word we know as a measure of liquid, and in keeping with the talk of 'drunkards' earlier in the speech. So much might be inferred without an appeal to the historical evidence, but the phrase 'of a doubt' still seems to throw the sentence out of gear. If we can satisfy ourselves that the obscurity is not due either to elliptical phrasing or to archaic usage, there remains another alternative: that there is an error in the text as it stands. Evidently the unintelligibility of this sentence takes us much further into the realms of hypothesis, and when we have begun to question the reliability of the text we are using, we are appealing to a different kind of historical evidence from that which refers to linguistic change.

The lines quoted above were taken from a modern edition of the play; the spelling is modern except for the word 'eale', which suggests that the editor is doubtful whether it does simply mean 'ale'. If we were to pursue the problem of understanding this last sentence, we should have to enquire where he derived his version of the text. We realize how dependent we are upon the editor's skill in presenting a reliable text. If his edition is accompanied by a full scholarly apparatus, of course, it will tell us on what earlier version or versions of the play he is basing his own text, on what principles he has chosen them, and on what principles he has made any alterations to them; he should also let us know whenever he has done this. We could then see whether the last sentence of Hamlet's speech is accurately presented in our text, and whether the error (if this is what we suspect) goes back to whatever text of the play is the ultimate source of our modern edition. In this case we should learn that there are no less than three early texts of *Hamlet* from which all others are derived, conventionally known as First Quarto (Q1) Second Quarto (Q2), and First Folio (F1), that the speech we are concerned with occurs only in Q2, and that our modern editor has accurately represented its reading of this final sentence.

Our enquiry into the meaning of Hamlet's words has thus opened up a whole area of historical reference, and if we are still persuaded that the source of our problem is an error of some kind, assuming that there was originally an intelligible 'correct' version of these lines which was accidentally altered or corrupted somewhere between the author and Q2, then our pursuit has not ended. For lack of further evidence, however, it has probably reached as far as we can take it. We have stirred up a kind of editorial hornet's nest: why is the speech only in Q2 and not in the other earliest texts? What is the relationship between these texts? Are they equally independent versions of the same play, of some single perfect copy of *Hamlet*? Is one or more of the three based upon any of the others? Is there such a thing as the play of *Hamlet*, or are there really three different *Hamlets* of which all later editions are a compound mixture? We leave these bewildering possibilities to braver souls, fervently acknowledging the soundness of that principle which states that only in the very last resort should unintelligibility be attributed to textual corruption, but still convinced that Hamlet's 'dram of eale' cannot be explained in any other way. Historical considerations in this case have not given us the meaning of the words, but they seem the only way of accounting for their lack of meaning.

Like the iceberg that shows only a fraction of itself above the surface, the obscurities that we recognize in the language of this speech should alert us to the possibility that there are some areas of meaning lost to a modern reader even where no difficulties are apparent. The lines, 'By the o'ergrowth of some complexion,/Oft breaking down the pales and forts of reason', for instance, make sense of a kind, once the glossary has told us that 'pales' means 'fences, barriers'. The mere ability to read English then suggests that the lines refer to some disorder affecting the reason. 'Complexion' is a word we may feel unsure of, but at least the context warns us that it is unlikely to refer merely to the condition of the skin on the face. In this case an historical approach to meaning serves to clarify and add precision to an idea that is vaguely comprehensible: the frame of reference is primarily that of the physio-psychological notions current when *Hamlet* was written (and for a very long time before): in the complexion, or complex, of the humours which determined a man's temperament, an excessive growth of one humour could disturb the temperamental stability and so threaten the mind. Reason, the power of judgment and understanding (not merely the logical capacity) was conceived of as the king or governor of the mind and body: 'that noble and most sovereign reason', in Ophelia's phrase. Hence the metaphors of military defence, and the suggestion of an insurrection in these lines. The conception of the body, or person, as a little kingdom, and conversely of the kingdom as a living organism, the 'body politic', is one of the commonplaces of Elizabethan thought, and illustrates the tendency of the age to think in terms of analogies and correspondences. Such correspondences are the basis of many of Shakespeare's metaphors, as here.

The speech as a whole moves from the state to 'particular men' on this same analogy. Similarly the Ghost is to tell Hamlet later in this scene that 'the whole ear of Denmark/Is by a forged process of my death/Rankly abused', before he proceeds to describe how 'the leprous distilment' was poured 'in the porches of my ears'. The rottenness in the state of Denmark is a reflection of the secret murder, the poisoning of the King, and the analogy between man and state holds true in a very special sense for the king, who embodies the state. It is an analogy which therefore lies at the basis of the whole play. Hamlet speaks here of the overthrow of reason in 'particular men' in terms of an insurrection or violent usurpation; he is about to learn, and so are we, of the manner in which his father's crown was usurped, by poison poured in the ears, and the Ghost himself uses the same terms figuratively to describe how the usurper has also poisoned the mind of a nation. But supposing it is the Ghost itself that is 'rankly abusing' Hamlet? Later in the play, Hamlet does become aware of this possibility, that perhaps the Ghost 'abuses me to damn me'. And so we have the attempt to discover 'grounds more relative' for Claudius's guilt, in the play-within-the-play. This begins with a dumb-show in which a king is poisoned through his ear while asleep in his orchard: what is it we are seeing in the dumb-show? The re-enactment of the murder of Hamlet's father? It corresponds closely to the circumstances revealed by the Ghost. Or an image of the poisoning of the mind by false report, the overthrow of reason while it is asleep and off its guard?

If the evidence of the play alone is not sufficient for us to recognize the essential ambiguity of the Ghost (and the way it is regarded by everybody who encounters it in the opening scenes puts it in a highly speculative context), then all the historical evidence we can muster about contemporary attitudes to supernatural apparitions supports Shakespeare's treatment of it as a subject for belief or doubt rather than certain knowledge. Hamlet decides to test the truth of the Ghost's story by means of another story, the Murder of Gonzago: again, Hamlet's stratagem, like the Ghost, depends upon how people (and one in particular) will respond, not upon whether it is true. Bearing in mind the play's earlier use of the analogies between man and the state, between reason and kingship, it is surely significant that dumb-shows in Elizabethan drama before *Hamlet* were usually figurative, emblematic devices, not literal summaries of the plot. The first dumb-show in the early Elizabethan tragedy of *Gorboduc*, for instance, is described in the play as follows:

> First, the music of violins began to play, during which came in upon the stage six wild men, clothed in leaves. Of whom the first bare in his neck a fagot of small sticks, which they all, both severally and together, assayed with all their

strength to break; but it could not be broken by them. At
the length, one of them pulled out one of the sticks and
brake it, and the rest, plucking out all the other sticks one
after another, did easily break them, the same being severed
which, being conjoined, they had before attempted in vain.
After they had this done, they departed the stage, and the
music ceased. Hereby was signified that a state knit in unity
doth continue strong against all force, but, being divided, is
easily destroyed; as befell upon Duke Gorboduc dividing his
land to his two sons, which he before held in monarchy, and
upon the dissension of the brethren, to whom it was divided.

'Hereby is signified': if the dumb-show in the Murder of
Gonzago is interpreted according to this convention, then, the
poisoning of a king through his ear takes on another meaning.
The modern reader is not likely to see the ambiguity if he only
understands the dumb-show as a shortened version of the play
it introduces; Claudius, on the other hand, is unlikely to take
offence at the dumb-show (and he seems not to do), if he
understands it figuratively. Thus different kinds of historical
evidence are not only mutually supporting but enable us to
see how the parts of the play are related to each other.

The ambiguous world of *Hamlet*, the doubtful and enig-
matic appearances that express a profound scepticism concerning the very foundation of human values, give the play a strong
appeal to the modern sensibility, as recent interpretations in
criticism and on the stage have shown. Its insistence upon the
frailty and limitations of human nature, and its questioning of
the moral basis for action, strike a responsive chord in what
we often think of as our own disillusioned and disoriented time.
Hamlet's reference to the great Renaissance commonplaces on
the glory of man, 'What a piece of work is a man', and his
ironic deflation of these claims, 'the beauty of the world! the
paragon of animals! And yet to me, what is this quintessence
of dust?' is an attitude that we feel, perhaps all too readily,
able to identify with. Thus we, like 'guilty creatures, sitting at
a play,/Have by the very cunning of the scene/Been struck so
to the soul that presently/[We] have proclaim'd [our] malefac-
tions.' It is part of the meaning of the play that we should
discover ourselves through it, but surely not in the sense that

we find it merely confirms our own preconceptions of ourselves. It is more challenging and therefore more valuable to us than this.

Hamlet's observation to Rosencrantz and Guildenstern, 'There's nothing either good or bad, but thinking makes it so', sounds like the very epitome of moral relativism in the play, the denial of an ultimate basis for value, which is likely to appeal to modern pragmatism. Certainly the line is an evasive mocking retort to his two inquisitors, but the line also carries a significant irony, which we shall see more certainly through an historical understanding. In the first place, the Elizabethan 'but' often means 'unless', and so in this sentence gives us a conditional clause rather than an antithesis. Moreover, since Hamlet's conception of man, as we have seen, is firmly rooted in those Renaissance orthodoxies which make 'godlike reason' the supreme authority in his state, it is indeed true that 'thinking', the exercise of conscience and reason, identifies good and bad. Hamlet's scepticism does not arise from doubt in the existence of ultimate values, but from the evidence only too close at hand that reason's sovereignty may be overthrown by the 'o'ergrowth of some complexion'.

Hamlet never doubts his obligation to heroic action, to the vengeance he has sworn; it is Claudius's guilt he needs to prove, not the moral justification for revenge. His problem is to reconcile the heroic duty with a very unheroic sense of human weakness. He is deeply aware of the instability and insecurity of the human condition; indeed, in the soliloquy 'To be or not to be', it is in this sense of insecurity, 'the dread of something after death', which he sees as the very basis of continued existence, 'the respect/That makes calamity of so long life'. But paradoxically when he comes to the lowest point of Fortune's wheel (the frequency with which the vicissitudes of Fortune are referred to in *Hamlet* reflects the shaping influence of this traditional concept in the play), and is being led away as Claudius's prisoner to the end that has been arranged for him in England, Hamlet then discovers that in the frailty and infirmity of man lies the very condition of heroic achievement. He sees Fortinbras's army on their quixotic adventure, and reflects upon Fortinbras,

Whose spirit, with divine ambition puff'd
Makes mouths at the invisible event,
Exposing what is mortal and unsure
To all that fortune, death, and danger, dare,
Even for an eggshell.

Hamlet's admiration of Fortinbras may strike us as mis-placed, but, as always, it is in the application to his own circumstances that we find the point of this speech. Since what is 'mortal' is also 'unsure', the heroic commitment is to accept the risk, to hazard all. This, although he did not then know it, was what Hamlet did in first accepting the Ghost at his word, and again in the play scene when he determined the King's guilt on similarly ambiguous evidence. Now he realizes the nature of heroic action, in terms of that incertitude and vulner-ability of man's lot which previously had seemed to deny the heroic possibility.

The sea-journey follows, and historical criticism will re-cognize that this emblem of the sea, part of the common property of the age which Shakespeare made peculiarly his own, itself expresses the hazards and uncertainties of human life. Hamlet returns from a direct confrontation with 'all that fortune, death, and danger, dare', as many critics have noted, a changed man. The graveyard scene, in which we first see Hamlet on his return, gains a special resonance from its echoes of traditional medieval attitudes to death. Death the Great Leveller is reflected in the social criticism directed at the court by these plebeian gravediggers, and in their lack of respect for the values and distinctions which count there, as well as in Hamlet's wry speculations on what has become of the great heroes, Alexander and Julius Caesar. Death the Jester is there too in the gravediggers' wit, and in that traditional grotesque emblem of the grinning skull, the *memento mori* which in this case belongs to the jester Yorick. The scene assumes a context of such familiar associations – familiar, that is, at the time it was written – as though these great commonplaces are being called upon to mock the heroic pretensions of man. Here Hamlet does see 'that undiscover'd country, from whose bourn/ No traveller returns', and this image, from the earlier soliloquy 'To be or not to be', can be recalled to relate Hamlet's sea-journey to this scene in the graveyard: both are confrontations with Death. And although the graveyard scene seems in one way to confirm the futility of heroic achievement, nevertheless the traveller has returned, and the image that was used to describe Fortinbras's heroism is echoed by the macabre wit and the grinning skull that visibly 'makes mouths at the invisible event'.

So Hamlet moves into the final scenes of the play, with that peculiar buoyancy which is neither flippant nor wearily resigned:

> If it be now, 'tis not to come; if it be not to come, it will be now; if it be not now, yet it will come – the readiness is all. Since no man owes of aught he leaves, what is't to leave betimes? Let be.

The difference between the question 'To be or not to be' and this affirmation 'Let be' is the measure of Hamlet's change. Now ' 'tis no matter' 'how ill all's here about my heart', not because his duty to heroic action or life itself have become matters of indifference, but because the hazards that make human enterprise so vulnerable are also the conditions of its value. If a man's life is more than sleeping and feeding, and Hamlet has always believed it should be, then it derives heroic meaning and worth from being staked on some great argument, from being totally at risk, morally, spiritually, and physically, in a cause not of its own making. Hamlet accepts the terms of such a life, and appropriately the duel in the final scene is fought for a royal wager, 'where honour's at the stake'.

The uncommitted anti-hero who is often represented as the Hamlet of our time is therefore not the Hamlet of the play. 'One can only perform one of several *Hamlets* potentially existing in this arch-play,' writes Jan Kott, 'It will always be a poorer *Hamlet* than Shakespeare's *Hamlet* is; but it may also be a *Hamlet* enriched by being of our time. It *may*, but I would rather say – it *must* be so.' What historical criticism tries to discern, on the other hand, is the *Hamlet* relevant to us precisely because it is released from mere contemporaneity. Such a *Hamlet* is indeed 'for all time'.

# 4

# English Studies and European Culture

*Gabriel Josipovici*

No one has ever doubted that English culture forms a part of European culture. There have been moments of nationalist fervour, such as the Elizabethan age or the period of the ballad revival in the late eighteenth century, when Englishmen stressed their native heritage and derided the popularity of Italian melodrama or classical mythology, but the very self-consciousness of such movements is the best proof of the fact that Englishmen have always regarded their literary and cultural heritage as stretching back into a common European past and outward into a common European present. For what is Old English poetry except one branch of Germanic heroic poetry? What is Middle English poetry except one branch of Christian European art? How else can one describe the poetry of Wordsworth and Shelley, of Eliot and Auden, except as part of European Romanticism and European Modernism? It is true that English literature has evolved according to its own native laws to a greater extent than the literature of France or Italy; it is true that there has always been a time-lag between artistic developments on the Continent and in the British Isles greater than can be accounted for simply by the size of the Channel. But no one would question the fact that Machaut was a greater influence on Chaucer than was Langland; Ariosto a greater influence on Spenser than was Chaucer; Cervantes a greater influence on Sterne than was Defoe; Dante and Laforgue greater influences on Eliot than were Tennyson or Arnold. And until the present century there have been few English writers who have not been familiar with the Hebrew Bible and the Greek and Latin classics, whatever their attitudes to their European contemporaries. It would seem perfectly natural then that the study of English at university should take account of these facts and ensure that the distortion of perspective which would inevitably result from the teaching of English literature in isolation be avoided at all costs. This has not, however, been the case in the past, and the reasons for this, whether hidden or overt, are particularly interesting. It may be useful to begin by examining some of the *disadvantages* of studying English in the context of European culture.

## The disadvantages of studying English in a European context

There is, to begin with, the problem of language. The growth of the study of English coincided with the decline of the study of Latin. The two phenomena are intimately related. From the Renaissance to the late nineteenth century the academic study of literature was the study of the Greek and Latin classics, and it was conducted – though with declining fervour – in Latin. The growth of English as an academic discipline is the growth of the recognition of the vernacular and the contemporary vernacular in particular, as a valid object of study.[1] The battle between Ancients and Moderns is as old as the Renaissance itself, and one episode in that battle is embodied in vernacular English literature as the Appendix to Swift's *Tale of a Tub*. But the result of the battle in the present century was that the rise of the study of modern vernacular literature led to the decline of classical studies. The modern student of English is thus rarely trained in the classics, and only rarely feels sufficiently at home in another European tongue to be able to master its literature. If, through some accident, such as having lived abroad, he can do this, then he usually opts for a degree in modern languages. Thus to try and integrate English studies into a European context means, for all practical purposes, asking students to read non-English literature in translation.

Clearly it is better to read Dante and Virgil in translation than not to read them at all. On the other hand, unless there is some awareness of what gets lost in translation, this method presents some very real dangers. And, strange as this may seem, the greatest of these is the danger that the work will be *too easily assimilated*.

Let us examine what this means. We all know the present vogue for 'modern' translations of the great European classics – Homer, Virgil, Horace, Dante. Some of these translations are extremely good. All of them encourage people to buy and read works they would probably never otherwise have tackled. And yet the very nature of their success is a gauge of the danger I have mentioned. For the fact is that Homer and Virgil and Horace and Dante are *not* modern. In a way one could say they were important to us precisely because they are not modern, precisely because they are *other*, they are all that we are not. Although no one today would want to be the Renaissance schoolboy toiling day in day out over Cicero and Seneca, that schoolboy had an awareness, as the modern reader of Day Lewis's translation of Virgil or Ciardi's translation of Dante has not, that these were difficult poets, hard writers who had put a lifetime's effort into their work and would give a lifetime's reading to the diligent reader.

The last thing I want to suggest is that all easy books are bad and that there is virtue in mere difficulty. I am not at all sure that an 'easy' book like Evelyn Waugh's *Decline and Fall* is not superior to *Finnegans Wake* or to Thomas Mann's *Lotte in Weimar*. What I do want to suggest is that the very availability of the great classics in good modern translations, the very proliferation of paperback editions of every single 'great book' in the world, can drug us into an unresponsive assimilation, a blurring of the very real differences between these books and the latest piece of English fiction. Everyone who has spent some time in one of the larger paperback bookshops in the country must have experienced that sinking feeling in the pit of the stomach, that vertigo and nausea in the face of so much literature, all there, all available, all, in the end, very much the same . . . For there is a satiety of the intellect as well as of the stomach.

One can of course argue that the same problem arises in the reading of the English classics, also available in good modern paperback editions. But here the differences in the language, however small, between even a Victorian novel and a contemporary one, will always remain as a built-in safe-guard against too easy an assimilation. We will always feel that we are reading the works of a particular individual, Dickens, or Trollope or Thackeray, with his own voice, his own turn of phrase, his own very individual *breath*. And we will unconsciously come to respect this voice, to listen to it and for it and eventually come to recognize it for what it is: the living speech of a man who miraculously lives in us through his books. But reading European literature in modern translation we may too readily see in it nothing but a reflection of ourselves, and therefore get precisely nothing out of it except the satisfaction of having 'got through' one small portion of all the literature that is available.

But can this be avoided? Is it even desirable that it be avoided? Do we not always read the literature of the past only for that which is directly relevant to ourselves now, today? There is a philosophical school, which we might term the historicist school, which argues that since we are living in the present, it is only 'in the present' that we can understand the literature of the past. It is no use asking: 'What does this or that book really mean?' since we can never discover the nature of that 'really'. We can only ask: 'What does this mean to me?' Only by facing this fact, the historicist argues, can we get rid of the dead weight of past authority and make use of the literature of the past for our present-day needs; only in this way can literature be taken out of the hands of those established in power and be used as the instrument of freedom and liberation it really is.

Like most extreme arguments this one contains a partial truth, which it distorts by presenting it as the whole truth. To read Cicero and Virgil merely because it is supposed to be 'good for one' is obviously pernicious. But is the alternative to select only those bits of Cicero and Virgil which immediately appeal? Because *we* believe that truth to love is of far greater value than fidelity to marriage vows should we therefore side entirely with Paolo and Francesca and condemn the Dante who condemns them? Because *we* find it easier to conceive of a world dominated by evil than of one in which spontaneous goodness will occasionally rise up to resist that evil should we read *King Lear* as a Renaissance version of Beckett's *Endgame*?[2] If we reply in the negative to all these questions and point out that we must try to read the literature of the past in the spirit in which it was written, the historicist will argue that we are not really reading literature at all. We are merely substituting certain ideas about Dante or Shakespeare for a true response to the text. But the historicist does not really go far enough. To his question: 'What can we know about the literature of the past since we can never emerge from the prejudices of our own age?', we may reply: 'What do you call the past? Five hundred years? One hundred years? Fifty? Ten? Five? One year? Ten minutes? One minute?' To put these questions to him is to recognize that what he is arguing for is not the impossibility of bridging the gap between *cultural epochs*, but between *any two people*. It is not just the past that I cannot understand except in my (limited and prejudiced) present terms, but any form of communication that I cannot understand except in my (limited and prejudiced) private terms. It looks as if the premises of the historicist drive one back into a complete solipsism, a total relativism, which has dogged philosophy almost from its beginnings, and to which one of the earliest answers was also one of the best. The whole of Socrates' philosophy seems to be an attempt to answer just such arguments by showing, among other things, that if we use language at all it is because some degree of agreement as to meaning is possible among people. Of course there will always be those for whom anything less than *total* communication is unbearable, and who would therefore have none at all rather than only a partial and limited form of communication. Indeed, much of the most significant literature of the last century and a half has sprung from just such an impulse, and I will have more to say about that later. But for the moment it is important to note that since literature uses language, and since language depends on some degree of social agreement, it can never be either totally assimilated or totally misunderstood. And this is true of today's newspaper as it is of Cicero or Virgil.

Perhaps, though, it is the function of art to force us out of our solipsism, to make us understand what it is like to be *other*, and that in this way art differs significantly from other forms of communication. If this is so, then one of the dangers of using modern translations in the academic study of literature

E

is that one loses just this sense of otherness, that one is confirmed in the solipsist position even more strongly than if one had never read more than one line in the original of Dante or Virgil. One of the essential functions of culture, which is to make us understand our past, rather than simply accepting it, or trying to overthrow it, is then in danger of dissolving as past and present merge. It is no coincidence that the extreme historicist position taken up by Heidegger and his pupils coincides in time with the growth of the paperback industry, which is busily feeding modern translations of the European classics to readers avid for culture. From a certain point of vantage one can see that these are two sides of the same coin.[3]

Having examined this first danger at some length we can now deal with the second a little more quickly. In any case, it is really only a variant on the first. Any attempt to deal with more than one literature in a university course makes it inevitable that a choice, a rigorous selection of which books are to be studied, will have to be made. Instead of following a national literature through from its origins to the present day, as one would do if studying only one literature, one is forced to study by means of what the Americans have aptly named a 'great books course'. This involves studying (always in translation, of course), a number of the great books of the Western world, from the *Iliad* to *The Magic Mountain*, via for example, *Oedipus Rex*, St Augustine's *Confessions*, *The Divine Comedy*, *Phèdre*, and *Wilhelm Meister*. The dangers inherent in such an approach are obvious. In the first place, who makes the selection? If it is the faculty of the University, they are then put in the position of having to *defend* their choices, an absurd way to approach literature. If it is the student, then he will naturally choose what has the most immediate appeal, which will be what fits in with ideas he already has, and he will lose the benefit of coming into contact with new ideas. At any rate it will lead to all the anguish of choosing between largely unknown quantities, with the consequent feeling that he should perhaps have chosen differently. Secondly, and more important, this principle of a 'great books course' has the effect of neutralizing to some extent what any one author is saying. If you take a book and are told to analyse it; if you are told, moreover, that it is one of the masterpieces of European culture; then the temptation is very strong to look for special, *aesthetic* criteria, which will validate such a judgment. We all know the tedium of those critical books which go into endless detail about the patterns and relationships within a single work of art, as if this was somehow the *reason* for its greatness.[4] Instead of reading it as the statement of a man, or a period, something that might affect our lives if we respond to it, we adopt the attitude of the *connoisseur* towards it. We learn to move among the master-pieces of the past without fear of being touched by them, picking one up here, putting another down there, praising the beauty of each, but totally dead inside to whatever any of them might be saying. The 'great books course', ideally conceived to bring culture to everyone, can easily turn us all into little frozen *connoisseurs*, able to talk about everything but responding to nothing. For, even more than reading the classics in translation without ever tackling the originals, to read only a choice of great books without reference to the authors or to the age from which they spring is to shut out the claims that others make upon us and to retreat even deeper into the solipsistic 'I'.

## Advantages of a purely English course

In the face of this the advantages of a university course where the subject studied is nothing but English are obvious. Added to it is the peculiar richness and continuity of the native tradition, so well described by Sir Maurice Powicke:

> We mean [he writes in *Medieval England*] that there is a con-tinuity, rarely to be seen elsewhere, in English history. Pro-perly speaking, there is no medieval and no modern history of England: there is just English history. We have had none of those revolutions which make a cleavage between past and present, and are, in the words of the poet, 'as lightning to reveal new seasons'. From time to time we have suffered – suffered terribly – but our land has never been devastated as France and Germany, Italy and Spain have been devastated. Our laws and language have grown and changed con-tinuously and almost imperceptibly. Many of the institutions and local divisions, here and there the actual buildings and agricultural arrangements of Saxon, Norman, Plantagenet

times are still with us – so that, though we know it not, we
are in a medieval world. There is a common humanity in our
literature, so that Chaucer's pilgrims, the noblemen, clowns,
and rustics in Shakespeare's plays, all the people in the
*Pilgrim's Progress*, the circle of Sir Roger de Coverley and
the ghostly villagers in Gray's 'Elegy', form one big company with the characters in the novels of Miss Austen and
Dickens. They are intelligible people: we understand them,
and they seem, as it were, to be speaking to us . . .

Everyone who has wandered much about England cannot
fail to have been moved by the sense of unity in English
history, for our history has been caught and retained by the
country-side, so that an English country-side is a harmonious
blending of nature and the works of men. And if he uses his
imagination in reflecting upon what he feels and observes,
the wanderer cannot but be impressed by the unceasing
receptivity of England on the one hand, and by her insular
tenacity on the other. The English have absorbed all varieties
of foreign influence, yet hitherto they have never been dis-
turbed by them. English history, like the English country, is
full of foreign things; they abound, yet they have ceased to
be foreign and are part of England; so that even the barrows
or burial-places of early man or Germanic kings, even Stone-
henge from prehistoric times and the walls of Pevensey from
Roman times add a quality always new and subdued to a
harmony of tone and to a beauty which have grown old
with them.

This was written in 1931 and I doubt if Powicke would feel so
confident today about the intelligibility of the characters of
Chaucer or Dickens, or about the peaceful and harmonious
character of the English countryside. And yet even in these last
forty or so years things have changed less than we are sometimes led to imagine. In one of his letters Keats writes: 'I like,
I love England. I like its living men. Give me a long brown
plain . . . so I may meet with some of Edmund Ironside's
descendants. Give me a barren mould, so I may meet with
some shadowing of Alfred in the shape of a gipsy, a huntsman
or a shepherd. Scenery is fine – but human nature is finer – the
sward is richer for the tread of a real nervous English foot.'

And this love of the land for itself and for its history can still be seen in writers as diverse as John Cowper Powys, T. H. White, even William Golding, who can hardly be characterized as sheltering from the burdensome present in an idealized past. It is even possible, in present-day industrial Britain, to go from one end of the island to the other on foot and keeping off the roads, as John Hillaby did in the summer of 1967 and recorded in his delightful *Journey Through Britain*. What is important for us, however, is the fact that English literature, of all the Western vernaculars, stretches in a virtually unbroken line from 650 to the present day. To study this literature historically is to be made aware of the ways a national literature can mature and develop, and of the ways in which a literature is always bound to a living language. A work such as C. S. Lewis's *Studies in Words* shows this approach at its best. Here the semantic study of language and the changing meanings of words such as 'silly' or 'good' reveals to us the changing nature of the civilization and makes us aware of the nature of the very tools we now use in daily speech. Because English is made up of so many diverse elements – Anglo-Saxon, Scandinavian, Latin, French – the study of the language is not only fascinating in itself, but it is also closely related to the social and political changes the country has seen in its long history. The study of the literature of England cannot be divorced from the study of the changing nature of the language, and both are clearly related to the institutions of the country. Thus to spend three years at university studying all this in some depth is not only to understand the otherness of the past, but also its present relevance. It is – or would seem to be – to become truly cultured.

## The disadvantages of a purely English course

I have been arguing a case for limiting the study of literature to English by pointing out first that no one has ever questioned the fact that English culture is a part of European culture, but that from this it does not necessarily follow that English literature ought to be supplanted or even supplemented at university level by the study of European literature. Indeed, I have argued, there are crucial disadvantages in doing this, as well as enormous advantages to be gained from a thorough and historical study of English literature in its social and historical context. Having done this I should like, for the rest of this chapter, to consider some of the disadvantages of such an approach, and to ask whether it is not possible to study English in the context of European culture while avoiding some of the pitfalls I have outlined above.

The main disadvantage of a purely English course is the distortion of perspective which this involves. There is no real danger of our failing to see that Spenser was influenced by Ariosto, or Milton by Virgil, or Pope by Horace. These influences spring at us out of their works, and English studies have always been aware – perhaps too aware – of their importance. No. What I am thinking of is something much less easy to define, a much subtler distortion. One so subtle, in fact, that it tends to pass unnoticed. And therein lies the danger. It is not just that there is a tendency to forget that so much of what was written and read in England until the eighteenth century was written in Latin (and printed on the continent, so that even catalogues of all the books printed in this country give one little or no idea of what was being read); it is not just that from 1066 to the middle of the fourteenth century the official language of England was French. It is that we inevitably tend to regard those areas of English literature which most clearly reflect English culture as being at the core of the English tradition. And those areas are of course the novel of the eighteenth and nineteenth centuries, with its freedom from the constraints of genre and its minute depiction of English society as it found it. This distortion of perspective does not affect poetry so much as fiction, and it does not affect those writers who are most obviously working in a European tradition, such as Spenser and Milton, since it is easy to see that they need to be understood within the context of those traditions. But it does affect those authors who appear to be working in a native tradition, such as Chaucer, Shakespeare, and Sterne. There is a strong built-in tendency to read these writers as approximating more or less closely to the norms of the nineteenth-century realist novel, a tendency which has been wittily described as the notion that 'all literature aspires to the condition of *Middlemarch*'.

Let us look first at the example of Chaucer. It has long been customary to see Chaucer as standing at the source of the English literary tradition, and to see him, with Shakespeare and Dickens, as one of the great 'English' writers. The great medievalist, W. P. Ker, was able to make the following statement about Chaucer's own development:

> Chaucer's whole literary career shows him emerging from the average opinion and manner of his contemporaries, and coming out from the medieval crowd to stand apart by himself, individual and free.

Other scholars have endorsed this picture, and have given it more body, by distinguishing three periods in Chaucer's development: an early period, which is French and conventional; a middle period, which is Italian and a little more realistic; and the final flowering of his genius in which he reveals himself as English and thoroughly earthy and realistic. Compared to his mature earthy realism, as exemplified in the Wife of Bath, we are told, the art of the rest of the Middle Ages reveals its aridity, its asceticism, its artificial and conventional nature.

But is this picture accurate? Recent studies have shown that Chaucer's 'realism', no less than his 'idealism' as exemplified by the Knight's and Squire's Tales, is traditional and conventional in character.[5] The descriptions of the characters in the General Prologue of the *Canterbury Tales*, far from being individuating and 'novelistic', are now seen to be a careful blend of type and detail, with a cunning use of iconographical motifs as rich in conventional associations as those of Dante and Langland. The Wife of Bath herself presents her case with such a dazzling array of Biblical references that we are at first disposed to take her at her face value; but we soon come to see that Chaucer is as ironic in his presentation of her as he is in his description of the Prioress, and that her parade of Scriptural authorities does more to condemn her in the eyes of the discerning reader than any of her actions.

But does this mean that we are now being presented with another Chaucer, better in some ways and less good in others, than the traditional image? I think not. What is happening is that we are learning to see Chaucer more clearly. We are learning that the conflict does not arise between originality and

convention, but between the good and bad *uses* of conventions
– or perhaps we could put it another way and say that it all
depends on whether a poet uses or is used by the conventions.
We can now see Chaucer's growing mastery, not as the shed-
ding of conventional elements, but as the mastery of conventions. If one compares, for instance, the *Troilus* of Chaucer
with his source in Boccaccio's *Filostrato,* we can see this
mastery at work. Boccaccio's poem is written according to the
conventions of courtly love: poet and reader accept these
conventions as do the characters. But Chaucer *uses* the conventions in order to make a point about the idealism of Troilus
alone. The narrator and Pandarus ensure that the audience
becomes aware of the fact that it is Troilus who conducts *his
life* according to certain poetic conventions which, because they
are not shared by the other characters, are seen to be arbitrary
and to some extent absurd. Thus when Troilus finds himself
for the first time alone (except for Pandarus) with his beloved,
he kneels down at her bedside and suddenly, overcome with
love, does what the code says he should and swoons. Were the
whole poem written within the conventions of the courtly code
we would simply accept this as natural and pass on. But this is
not Chaucer's method. At once Pandarus rushes forward,
admonishes Troilus for his act, strips him, and pushes him into
bed with Criseyde. At this point we feel the actual *weight* of
Troilus, the mass of his body, in a way we never do in Boccaccio. And the gap between the code and real life, the ideal and
the actuality, is brought home to us. Nor is Chaucer's point
simply that Troilus is wrong and Pandarus right; as we see
later on, the 'realism' of the latter is as limited as the 'idealism'
of the former. Out of the clash of the two the reader is forced
to recognize the clichés by which his own life is governed and
thus to some extent to free himself from their dominion. The
literary conventions, like the convention which is language,
allow Chaucer to develop his ironic tale, just as Shakespeare
will later make use of the conventions of his own day.

What the example of Chaucer reveals is not just the in-
adequacy of the old view, but the particular premises of that
view. These can be simply defined as those of a *cultural
Darwinism.* History, according to this view, moves forward and
upward, culminating in the present, and the arts follow the

same law. Like all theories this one has historical roots – in the rational positivism of the eighteenth and nineteenth centuries. Although two World Wars have revealed the absurdity of its liberal optimism, it still has a tenacious hold, especially in the field of art history. Ker's view of Chaucer's development is only one tiny example of it, but it permeates nearly all histories of literature and of the visual arts. Art historians are more aware of its dangers today than are historians of literature. The latter still tend to speak of medieval drama, for instance, as a poor forerunner of that of Elizabethan England, or of the prose of Nashe as a hesitant groping towards the form of the novel as found in Defoe or Richardson.[6]

Nashe provides a particularly interesting example. The most striking thing about his writing is the exuberance of his style, but when we ask what function this style has in his work we are usually given answers that start from the same premises as the traditional novel, which was not born till a hundred years after Nashe. Thus Ian Watt, in his *The Rise of the Novel*, one of the best-known books on the subject, writes:

> The previous stylistic tradition for fiction was not primarily concerned with the correspondence of words to things, but rather with the extrinsic beauties which could be bestowed upon description and action by the use of rhetoric.

But these terms – 'the correspondence of words to things', 'the extrinsic beauties . . . bestowed upon description' are clichés of the late seventeenth century, the product of that change of direction taken by European culture after the Renaissance, and of which the rise of science, the rise of the bourgeoisie, the development of Calvinism, are all aspects. The words of Ian Watt could have come out of the famous *History of the Royal Society* written in 1676 by Thomas Sprat, and they totally fail to account for Nashe's style. Nashe is not a bumbling forerunner of Defoe. He belongs to a European tradition far older than that of the novel, a tradition which goes back to Lucian in the second century A.D. and runs through Erasmus, Rabelais, Swift and Sterne, and into Joyce, Nabokov and Beckett in the present century. This is a tradition which is less interested in the presentation of character and society and more concerned with the problem of discourse itself: what happens to speech when it gets into books? What happens to words when they get into novels? What distortions inevitably occur when I put my life into a book? These questions, which worry writers like Rabelais and Sterne, do not seem to exist for the traditional novel, which complacently takes its own values for granted. But they are the very questions we have come to associate with *modern* fiction, with the anti-novel of Joyce or Beckett or Robbe-Grillet. The light-hearted jokes Sterne makes at the expense of a novelist like Richardson are just those which furnish Sartre with his strongest weapons when, in *La Nausée* and other early writings, he condemns the traditional novel for its 'bad faith'.

But if this is so then a very interesting point emerges. Perhaps the failure of the Anglo-Saxon academic world to come to terms with Modernism stems from the same source as its failure (until recent years) to come to terms with the Middle Ages, and with such writers as Nashe and Sterne. Both are the result of taking the traditional novel as the unquestioned norm and trying to assimilate all fiction to it. And this in turn is the result of the implicit acceptance of a cultural Darwinism which is directly related to the liberal positivism of the last part of the nineteenth century, which is the time when the academic study of English took root. And we are now beginning to see that the major critical books that have appeared in the last few years owe their breadth, their understanding of the many literatures of antiquity and of the Middle Ages, to a thorough assimilation of the lessons of Modernism. Let us glance at two of the greatest of these books: *Mimesis*, by Erich Auerbach, and *Anatomy of Criticism*, by Northrop Frye, for, among other things, what they impart is a notion of European culture.

### The notion of European culture

Auerbach was brought up in the old German philological tradition. He was a classicist and a medievalist by training, and, like so many others, he left his native Germany when the Nazis came to power. He wrote *Mimesis*, his greatest book, in Istanbul between 1942 and 1945. It is an attempt to explore the rendering of reality in European writing from Homer to Virginia Woolf. Auerbach's method is to take a short passage of prose or verse and subject it to minute syntactic analysis. In so doing he moves forward from the passage to its immediate context, from that to the wider context of the author's other works or those of contemporaries, and from that to the whole culture from which the passage sprang. Each chapter is thus a remarkable demonstration of the unity of form and content, not just in literature, but in historical writing, in chronicles, in autobiographies: the syntax is the age as the style is the man. In dealing with the Bible, Tacitus, Montaigne and Pascal, as well as Cervantes and Shakespeare and Goethe, Auerbach breaks down the barriers which academics have drawn up round the term 'literature' and shows us how closely all forms of discourse are linked to the ages that produced them. Naturally he is more revealing on ancient and medieval authors, not just because he is more familiar with them, but rather because his method, which is the absolute antithesis to the old biographical approach, is more suited to the anonymous author than to the one who deliberately tries to differentiate himself from his age – to find that 'subtler language' with which men, from the Renaissance, and especially from Romanticism onwards, have tried to express that which is unique to themselves.

Auerbach's method, however, as he himself says in his epilogue, was in part dictated by the fact that Istanbul during the war was not the best place to find the kind of technical literature he would have required had he been writing a more conventional kind of book:

> The lack of technical literature and periodicals may also serve to explain that my book has no notes. Aside from the texts, I quote comparatively little, and that little it was easy to include in the body of the book. On the other hand it is quite possible that the book owes its existence to just this lack of a rich and specialized vocabulary. If it had been possible for me to acquaint myself with all the work that has been done on so many subjects, I might never have reached the point of writing.

But earlier, in his chapter on Virginia Woolf, he remarked:

> There is greater confidence in syntheses gained through full

exploitation of an everyday occurrence than in a chrono-
logically well-ordered total treatment which accompanies the
subject from beginning to end, attempts not to omit anything that is externally important, and emphasizes the great
turning points of destiny. It is possible to compare this
technique of modern writers with that of certain modern
philologists, who hold that the interpretation of a few
passages from *Hamlet, Phèdre,* or *Faust* can be made to yield
more, and more decisive information about Shakespeare,
Racine, or Goethe and their times than would a systematic
and chronological treatment of their lives and works. Indeed,
the present book may be cited as an illustration . . .

Thus his book itself, he sees, could not have been written
without the examples of writers like Joyce and Virginia Woolf,
who break up strict chronology, and make all of the past
instantaneously present. But that is not its only link with this
century. Like the great synthesizing works of his art historian
contemporaries and fellow exiles, Auerbach is impelled to
examine the whole of Western culture as an act of faith and
piety in a time when that culture seemed on the point of being
engulfed by the barbarity of fascism. Writing in Istanbul as the
war draws to an end, Auerbach concludes his epilogue:

I hope that my study will reach its readers – both my friends
of former years, if they are still alive, as well as all the others
for whom it was intended. And may it contribute to bringing
together again those whose love for our western history has
serenely persevered.

*Anatomy of Criticism,* which was written by a Protestant
Canadian rather than a German Jew, and which came out in
1957, is a totally different kind of book. Nevertheless, the two
have much in common – or rather, they are complementary.
Frye argues that there comes a time in every discipline where
we cease to add yet more facts to those already existing, and
suddenly understand the laws underlying the individual facts.
He feels that the pragmatic approach to literature – 'one damn
book after another' – should give way to an approach which
recognizes that literature as a whole has a certain shape, is

governed by certain laws. The basic law is that of *displacement*: all literature is the displacement of a central myth which cannot be formulated except through such displacement. Seen in this way literature is no longer a series of objects but a set of forms. Frye thus sets out to write what might be called a generative grammar of literature, in the same way as linguists like Saussure and, more recently, Chomsky, have attempted to do for language itself. As Roland Barthes,[7] the French critic whose work bears many interesting resemblances to that of Frye, has said:

> Confronted with the impossibility of mastering all the phrases of a language, the linguist decides to set up a *hypothetical model of description*, whereby he can explain how the infinite phrases which make up a language are engendered.

In a similar way Frye endeavours to explain how the infinite works which make up the totality of literature are engendered. The effect of this is rather frightening. What we had thought of as a solid, stable object, is now seen to be only a form, what we had thought of as a 'given' is suddenly seen to be the result of certain kinds of assumptions, which vary from epoch to epoch and country to country. All art operates according to conventions, for it is the conventions that make communication possible, and the more an artist thinks he can do without these the more likely he is to fall a victim to them. The nineteenth-century novel, which imagined it was exploring the world around it or expressing the inmost feelings of the author, is seen to be full of the clichés of romance, the dark, passionate, evil heroine, for instance, as opposed to the fair, gentle, good heroine. As Frye remarks: 'When the two are involved with the same hero, the plot usually has to get rid of the dark one or make her into a sister if the story is to end happily. Frye's examples include Scott's *Ivanhoe*, Fennimore Cooper's *The Last of the Mohicans*, Wilkie Collins's *The Woman in White*, Edgar Allen Poe's *Ligeia*, Melville's *Pierre* (a tragedy because the hero chooses the dark girl who is also his sister), and Hawthorne's *The Marble Faun*.

Frye's book, as we have seen, has much in common with modern linguistics. It also has much in common with

Nietzsche, Freud and Mallarmé, for what it reveals is one of the key ideas behind modern developments in the arts and the social sciences, the idea that culture itself is not a 'given', but is man-made, and therefore to be explained by reference to men. As Nietzsche realized, the peculiar thing about man is that he is the only animal with a history. But there must be a reason for this, and Nietzsche suggests that what has driven civilization forward is a feeling of guilt which is initially repressed and projected outwardly, the projection then causing further repression, in an ever-increasing spiral. Civilization itself is thus seen to be a kind of dynamic displacement which engenders further displacement. In exactly the same way Freud saw the cycle occurring in the individual human being. At the same time artists began to see that the norms and forms they had inherited from the past did not correspond to reality itself, but were merely the spectacles through which it had been customary to see reality.

The great discovery of Modernism then is that the past is not a solid mass, weighing down on the present, but is itself in need of reinterpretation in terms of the present. The world is not 'like this'; it is only 'like this when I wear this particular set of spectacles'. In other words, the loss of belief in a transcendental authority eventually led, by the end of the nineteenth century, to a relativization of all facts. Nothing is given, all is in need of interpretation. It is no coincidence then that it is the Modernist movement in the arts which rediscovers the visual art and the poetry of the Far East, the sculpture of Africa, the songs of the Middle Ages, the music of India. Once the norms of the Renaissance and the seventeenth century were seen for what they were (only one of a possible set of conventions), it was possible to assimilate and employ art forms which had seemed brutish and barbarian to the eighteenth and nineteenth centuries. Modernism, as Eliot stressed again and again, is thus a rediscovery of the past, and Northrop Frye's book, so medieval in its organization, is, as he himself is the first to acknowledge, a product of the Modernist revolution. It is important precisely because it brings into the academy the central ideas of the moderns, ideas which, understandably, the academy has never been too willing to face up to.

## The academy and the market-place

Although the university as we know it dates from the Middle Ages, the academic study of literature dates from the Renaissance. The Renaissance is the first of the many European movements which are the result of a peculiar self-consciousness. When Machiavelli donned his Roman toga and retired into his library to read the books of the ancients, he acknowledged, for perhaps the first time, that books are something special, peculiar, apart. And of what use are books? They put us in touch with a past which is nobler than the present, with a classical past which we must strive to emulate. It is this view of culture which academics have seen it as their task to hand down from generation to generation, until we come to Arnold's *Culture and Anarchy*. And it is in reaction to this monolithic, static, and ultimately stultifying view of culture that the historicists I mentioned earlier were rebelling. They wanted none of this piety towards a dead past. In its place they wanted something which would speak to them, to their condition, rather than foisting upon them the assumptions and values of a patrician *élite*. Thus a polarization was set up, which we can see most clearly at certain periods of turmoil in the history of education, when the public divides into two camps, the conservative patrician academic *élite* and the radical historicist revolutionaries. Unfortunately, both positions involve a distortion of the complex truth.

The polarization is already there in the sixteenth century. For what else is the quarrel of Protestants and Catholics, except the struggle between those who will accept only their inner promptings and those who will accept only the authority of the Church? And, of course, the argument cannot be resolved on the premises of either side, for both oversimplify the relation between inner and outer, between spirit and letter, freedom and authority.[8] We have heard much recently of student revolutionaries and academic reactionaries; it is perhaps a slight comfort to realize that they were already deep in argument four hundred and fifty years ago.

When Machiavelli put on his toga to go into his study he became the symbol of a crucial change in European thought. As Panofsky has shown, the Middle Ages were not conscious

of classical antiquity because they were in a sense at one with
it.[9] That is why C. S. Lewis has felt that Gavin Douglas's translation of the *Aeneid* is closer to the original than is Dryden's
translation. When people start imitating classical antiquity it
means that they no longer feel at one with it – it is separate
from them, cut off by the darkness of the Middle Ages, that
Gothic and barbarian time. And this view of antiquity, as something different and worthy of imitation, is at the root of all
study of the humanities up to the present time. It is against
this that those rebel who would have us study nothing but the
contemporary and the immediately appealing. There is, however, another answer to the dilemma.

When Shakespeare uses classical myth he does it in a very
different way from Milton. With Milton it is a matter of conscious reconstruction. With Shakespeare the gods and god-
desses of antiquity are as present as the goblins and pucks of
an Elizabethan village. Milton's effort, throughout his life, is
to keep at bay the temptations of his native language and of
the local myths of England, to shield himself behind the barrier
of a latinized English and of a classical mythology. When
viewed in this light, all his major works can be seen as presenting, at the level of fiction, what is present at the level of the
poet's own stance. The temptation of the Lady in *Comus*, of
Adam, of Christ, of Samson, are all temptations to yield in
some way, and all except Adam reject the temptation through
an effort of the will, a steeling of the mind. For this reason we
can say that Milton is the first true Renaissance poet England
produced, a figure who, like Michaelangelo, finds his strength
in rejection, denial, and the deliberate imitation of the ancients.
In Shakespeare and the Elizabethans, on the other hand, as in
the poets of the Middle Ages, all is ease and assimilation, the
effortlessness of an art that is simultaneously sophisticated
and naïve.[10]

Milton's attitude, when divorced from his heroic vision and
his poetic genius, is the attitude of the academy. It is also the
attitude of the connoisseur, of the admirer of the beautiful who
is careful to see that the beautiful does not touch the deepest
springs of his own heart. It is the attitude of Swann, in Proust,
who admires all that the past has to offer in the way of lovely
things, admires but does not love. For to love means to give

yourself up to something, it means to lay yourself open to pain, to suffering, which is the mark of our emergence from the contemplation of our private egos. Marcel recognizes this as he recognizes that he must love Albertine in a different way from the way Swann loves his paintings:

> But no, Albertine was in no way a work of art. I knew what it meant to admire a woman in an artistic fashion. I had known Swann. For my own part, moreover, I was, no matter who the woman might be, incapable of doing so, having no sort of power of detached observation . . . The pleasure and the pain that I derived from Albertine never took, in order to reach me, the line of taste and intellect; indeed, to tell the truth, when I began to regard Albertine as an angel musician glazed with a marvellous patina whom I congratulated myself upon possessing, it was not long before I found her uninteresting; I soon became bored in her company, but these moments were of brief duration; we love only what we do not possess, and very soon I returned to the conclusion that I did not possess Albertine.

Two types of art are being contrasted here, and two types of love. The first, which sees *beauty* as the necessary condition, must have a prior set of criteria against which to match the work of art or the woman – only certain kinds of things can be called beautiful; and it guards the object as a precious possession, to be taken out occasionally and contemplated or shown with pride to others. The second, which has *truth* as its condition, strives to enter the otherness of the object while knowing that it can never fully do so. The first is, naturally enough, the method of the academy. Naturally, because the teacher almost of necessity has to neutralize the power of the object if he is to talk about it year in year out; to allow it the power of its otherness would create an intolerable situation. So that built in to the academic treatment of literature is the connoisseur approach, which is, by and large, the approach of the Renaissance to classical antiquity. But it is a falsification of the effects of art, as of life, as the young Marcel perceives. And this explains why artists have for so long felt that academics, however well-meaning and sympathetic, are of the devil's party, and that there must be no truck with them.

F

In contrast to the connoisseur mentality is that of the great modern artists, whose output can be seen as a series of raids upon the past in an effort to make that past their own without destroying its unique quality. One has only to think of Eliot's own forays, or of Picasso's extraordinary series of variations on Velasquez's *Las Meninas,* or a work such as Stravinsky's *Pulcinella,* of which the composer wrote:

> *Pulcinella* was my discovery of the past, the epiphany through which the whole of my late work became possible. It was a backward look, of course – the first of many love affairs in that direction – but it was a look in the mirror too. No critic understood this at the time, and I was therefore attacked for being a *pasticheur,* chided for composing 'simple' music, blamed for deserting 'modernism', accused of renouncing my 'true Russian heritage'. People who had never heard of, or cared about, the originals cried 'sacrilege': 'The classics are ours. Leave the classics alone.' To them all my answer was and is the same: You 'respect', but I love.

And what is love? It is the acknowledgment by the whole self of the otherness, the uniqueness of the thing loved, as well as the attempt to comprehend that otherness. In other words, it draws us out of our limited selves, and frees us from the tyranny of either the academy or the market-place, from seeing the past as either frozen and monolithic or as non-existent. And it is precisely this love for the past, for our heritage, that modern art, if we can but learn its lesson, can teach us.

### Culture and European culture

There are signs that the lesson has indeed been learnt. A number of impressive works of scholarship which have appeared in the last fifteen years have seen it as their task to recreate the past for us in such a way that we will be able to respond to it with a genuine understanding. The books of John Jones on Aristotle and Greek Tragedy, of V. A. Kolve on the medieval miracle plays, of C. S. Singleton on Dante, of A. C. Hamilton on Spenser, have all in some way restored the past to us while allowing it its singularity. These are genuine contributions because they do not conceive of culture as an *essence,* as something which we must hug to ourselves to protect ourselves from the philistines, but, on the contrary, as a widening of the horizons, a supplying of the right context in which to understand the past. What they are doing can be explained by an example which Frye gives of a problem of translation:

> It is impossible that a Greek tragedian can have meant by *ananke* what the average English reader means by 'necessity'. But the translator must use some word, and the real difficulty lies in the reader's inability to recreate the word 'necessity' into a conception with the associative richness of *ananke* ... Where are we to find the meanings of words? Sophocles is dead and eke his language, and both at once are buried in dictionaries which give only the translator's equivalent. The meaning of *ananke* must be sought in the meaning of the poetic form in which it is found, in the *raison d'être* of Greek tragedy. Here a knowledge of the historical origin and context of Greek tragedy is necessary, but . . . we must eventually move beyond this. Just as we must find the meaning of *ananke* in its relation to its context in Greek tragedy, so we must find the meaning of Greek tragedy in its relation to the context of all tragedy . . .

Thus, slowly and painfully, we can overcome the half-truths which say either that the past is irrecoverable or that we must accept what we are told about it.

We must not look at culture as an essence, a thing, but rather as the supplying of a context, the provision both of better spectacles, and of a sufficient variety of spectacles to keep us from forgetting that what we see is never seen by the unaided power of the eyes alone. Nearly all misinterpretations are the result of a failure to appreciate the context of a work of art, and for English literature that context must inevitably be European. But of course, as we have seen, just as there is no essence known as English culture, so there is no essence known as European culture. The term culture is itself an Enlightenment term in its modern connotations of tastefulness and civilization, and we can now see that it is nothing other than a mirror of the aspirations of the century itself. Each age of course recreates the past in its own image, but our awareness of this can allow us to try and nullify it. We can see now, through the work of recent critics as well as of men like Nietzsche, that Homer and the Greek tragedians and the authors of the Old Testament were very, very different from eighteenth-century English or German gentlemen. Can we say that they are European at all? But what does European mean? Do we have some set of characteristics which we try to relate to every work we encounter? The answer is that of course we don't. The confusion is somewhat like that which Wittgenstein discovered in the discussion of games. There are card games and ball games and other games such as tiddly-winks, which don't use either cards or balls. What unites all of them is not some essence of which they all partake, 'gameness', but rather certain overlapping characteristics, more akin to family resemblances. What is important is not to try and make all games look the same, not to see everywhere only our own reflections in the past. It is the otherness, the strangeness of Greek tragedy that John Jones stresses, and he rightly sees that the first condition of understanding it is an acknowledgment of this. In a similar way Robert Lowell[11] explains his love for the classics:

Before going to Kenyon I talked to Ford Madox Ford and Ransom, and Ransom said you've just got to take philosophy and logic, which I did. The other thing he suggested was classics. Ford was rather flippant about it, said of course you've got to learn classics, you'll just cut yourself off from humanity if you don't. I think it's always given me some sort of yardstick for English. And then the literature was amazing, particularly the Greek; there's nothing like Greek in English at all ... That something like *Antigone* or *Oedipus* or the great Achilles moments in the *Iliad* would be at the core of a literature is incredible for anyone brought up in an English culture – Greek wildness and sophistication all different, the women different, everything. Latin is of course much closer. English is a half-Latin language, and we've done our best to absorb the Latin literature. But a Roman poet is much less intellectual than the Englishman, much less abstract. He's nearer nature somehow ... And yet he's very sophisticated. He has his way of doing things, though the number of forms he explored is quite limited. The amount he could take from the Greeks and yet change is an extra-ordinary piece of firm discipline. Also, you take almost any really good Roman poet – Juvenal, or Virgil, or Propertius, or Catullus – he's much more raw and direct than anything in English, and yet he has this block-like formality. The Roman frankness interests me. Until recently our literature hasn't been as raw as the Roman, translations had to have stars. And their history has a terrible human frankness that isn't customary with us – corrosive attacks on the establishment, comments on politics and the decay of morals, all felt terribly strongly, by poets as well as historians. The English writer who reads the classics is working at one thing, and his eye is on something else that can't be done. We will always have the Latin and Greek classics, and they'll never be absorbed. There's something very restful about that.

## Conclusion

The reading of books does not automatically make us better people. Nor is that a reason for giving up the reading of books. There are right and wrong ways of doing most things, and reading is no exception. This is what the academic study of literature can teach us – not how to respond, which is a private matter between the reader and the book, but how to relate that response to the rest of one's life and reading. As Frye points out:

Physics is an organized body of knowledge about nature, and a student of it says he is learning physics, not nature. Art, like nature, has to be distinguished from the systematic study of it, which is criticism. It is therefore impossible to 'learn literature': one learns about it in a certain way, but what one learns, transitively, is the criticism of literature. Similarly, the difficulty often felt in 'teaching literature' arises from the fact that it cannot be done: the criticism of literature is all that can be directly taught.

To study English literature in the context of European culture is suddenly to begin to ask the right questions, to see its distance from us but also its contemporaneity – always pro-vided we remember that culture is not an essence but the provision of a sense of context. To do this is to make ourselves better readers of those authors who are most in need of readers: those who are writing today. To see English literature in the context of European culture is to be made aware that the past is not a crushing burden of authority, but the means of freeing us of our prejudices and habits. It is to take our place as responsible and responsive – that is, active – readers of modern literature. It is the least we can do.

## Notes

1. See Walter J. Ong, 'The Vernacular Matrix of the New Criticism', in *The Barbarian Within*, New York, 1962.
2. This last example is a reference to the Polish critic, Jan Kott, whose *Shakespeare our Contemporary* shows all the virtues and vices of the historicist position (see above, pp. 52–4). He gives a marvellous sense of Shakespeare's relevance, but at the cost of distorting a great deal of Shakespeare. Is there a less easy but more reliable path?
3. My discussion of the 'historicist' fallacy is greatly indebted to E. D. Hirsch's brilliant book, *Validity in Interpretation*, Yale University Press, 1967, especially Appendix II, pp. 245–64.
4. E. H. Gombrich, 'Raphael's Madonna della Sedia', in *Norm and Form*, London, 1965, deals with this problem in connexion with a famous painting and its commentators.
5. See especially Charles Muscatine, *Chaucer and the French Tradition*, Berkeley, California, 1957.
6. There is an enormous literature that could profitably be consulted here. See especially the works of Gombrich, in particular his early *History of Art* and *Art and Illusion*. On the medieval drama see V. A. Kolve, *The Play Called Corpus Christi*, London, 1967. Also useful is William Matthews's essay, 'Inherited Impediments in Medieval Literary History', in *Medieval Secular Literature*, ed. Matthews, Berkeley, California, 1965.
7. *Critique et vérité*, Seuil, Paris, 1966, p. 57.
8. See H. Popkin, *A History of Scepticism from Erasmus to Descartes*, Assen, 1960, especially Ch. I for the sixteenth-century crisis.
9. See especially three essays in *Meaning in the Visual Arts*, Doubleday Anchor Books, 1955: 'Iconography and Iconology', 'The first page of Giorgio Vasari's *Libro*' and 'Dürer and Classical Antiquity'.
10. I am indebted here to Mr A. D. Nuttall.
11. From an interview in the *Paris Review*, no. 25, Spring 1961.

# 5

---

# The Study of the
# English Language

*R. B. Le Page*

### Philology

In a number of British universities the establishment of English
language studies in an historical context preceded the modern
disciplines of literary criticism. Such studies were largely concerned with the recovery and publication of ancient texts in the
various Germanic languages, and with textual commentary and
elucidation. This kind of scholarship is known in European
(and often in American) universities as philology, and it was
the necessary base on which both historical linguistics and
literary criticism have built.

As an early example, in 1665 Francis Junius the younger and
his pupil Thomas Mareschall printed and published in Dor-
drecht their transcription of, and linguistic commentary on, the
four Christian gospels, giving parallel texts in Gothic and
Anglo-Saxon. The typefaces were designed by Junius himself
and beautifully cut so as to recreate as closely as possible the
appearance of the manuscript versions. My own copy of this
book has passed through the hands of a number of Germanic
philologists who have signed it on the title-page and annotated
it in the margin. It is bound together with the

GOTHICUM GLOSSARIUM
quo pleraque ARGENTEI   Codicis Vocabula
explicantur, atque ex Linguis cognatis illustrantur.
*Præmittuntur ei* GOTHICUM, RUNICUM, ANGLO-SAXONICUM,
aliáque *ALPHABETA*

75

These were compiled, once again, by Junius. Together the two volumes make up one thousand pages. They provided a text-book for seventeenth-century university students wishing to learn Gothic and Anglo-Saxon, to read some texts in these languages and to learn about runes. This was at a time when the study of early Germanic literature was in its infancy in Britain, following the partial recovery by private collectors of dispersed monastic libraries. The texts could be made very widely available in printed form once the process of transcription (which, in the case of damaged manuscripts, sometimes called for decipherment or reconstruction) had been done; the results of philological scholarship could thus be widely disseminated, and provided the basis for the antiquarian study of Germanic literature which then began for the first time to take its place by the side of classical studies in Hebrew, Greek and Latin.

Manuscripts in Anglo-Saxon (or Old English, as it is now more generally called) provide by far the largest body of vernacular literature in Western Europe for the period from the eighth to the eleventh centuries, long antedating literature in the Romance (as opposed to Latin) languages. In addition to the various portions of Biblical glossing, translation and commentary we have four major volumes of poetry (some of it of little literary value but some profoundly moving) and, among many other prose remains, sermons, biographies, books of travel and various versions of the Anglo-Saxon Chronicle. I am not concerned here with these books as literature, but mention them in order to convey something of the antiquarian and literary interests which inspired many of the early philologists. Above all, they were concerned to provide accurate texts on which literary and linguistic studies could be based.

In the eighteenth, nineteenth and twentieth centuries the work of the philologists has resulted in great numbers of texts being made freely available of which otherwise only a single or very few copies might remain. Frequently it has to be recognized that the surviving manuscripts, apart from being possibly defaced or damaged, are the end products of a long process of copying by one scribe after another in successive generations, so that editors sometimes attempt to reconstruct earlier and more 'authentic' versions.

In Britain the term *philology* has often been extended to include the linguistic studies which can be based upon such textual work – what is elsewhere called historical and comparative linguistics. The papers published nowadays in the *Transactions of the Philological Society* of London are concerned far more with linguistics than with textual work, and a recent paper defined philology as

> a predominantly historical and comparative approach, with the primary interest directed upon the historical derivation and the cognate affinities of linguistic items and sets of items (James Barr, in 'Semitic Philology and Linguistics', *Trans. Phil. Soc.*, 1968, p. 37).

(The American *Journal of English and Germanic Philology*, on the other hand, is primarily concerned with textual and literary 'explication'.) The great editors of such series as those of The Early English Text Society have been very far from philistines. Many of them, down to the present day, have shown a marked sensitivity of literary judgment. A basic requirement of their discipline however has been the rather difficult task of learning to read and understand ancient manuscripts written in languages which, although they bore some resemblance to modern English, were really quite distinct. Anglo-Saxon – a better name in some respects than Old English – is as distinct from modern English as modern German is.

Middle English – or English as it is used in manuscripts from about 1100 until about 1450 – is much better documented than Old English and not as remote from us linguistically. It is one of the most general results of contact between different language-communities that the emerging *lingua franca* is more analytical in its grammar than that of either of the languages before contact – supposing that one or both of these had had a synthesizing (or inflecting) grammar. As a result of a series of waves of invasion and colonization English-speakers were brought into contact, first with the Romano-British peoples whom they conquered, and then with the Vikings and Normans who in turn overran them. The succession of contact situations has been continued down to our own day as English has been carried overseas and creole varieties have emerged. At each stage in this history the remains of the inflectional system of

Old English have been further eroded. The Old English phrase *on wordum þæs cyninges* might be rendered in modern English as *in the king's words* or *in the words of the king*, and in broad Jamaican Creole as *iina di wod-dem fi di king*. Chaucer's English, reflecting the usage of educated people in London after three hundred years of Norman-French domination, is more like our own in this particular respect than it is like Old English, and once we have learned how to pronounce his verse and have grasped the meanings of his words, his language does not present very great difficulties.

Even in the treatment of Middle English and later texts, however, there is a great deal for the philologist to do, both as an editor and as an historian of the language. Poetry and prose in other dialects by Chaucer's contemporaries, for example, are further removed from our own usage, either because those dialects were more conservative – that is, less affected by Norman contact, closer to Old English in their structure – or because they had been affected by contact with other language-communities such as the Norse speakers. Thus the language of the poet of British Museum MS. Cotton Nero A.x., which contains the four poems known as *Sir Gawain and the Green Knight*, *Pearl*, *Cleanness* (or *Purity*) and *Patience*, contains not only a fairly large number of words of Norse origin not found in southern dialects but also some distinctive forms of the personal pronouns and of noun and verb inflexions.

These particular poems, like Chaucer's, were however intended for a courtly audience. A century earlier English had been little used for courtly poetry; what was written or composed in English was of a more homely nature, its language often more colloquial. Chaucer himself had a keen ear for the telling colloquialism, the appropriate proverb or cliché on the lips of one or other of his characters, and fewer inhibitions about the literary appropriateness of such language than, for example, his contemporary, Gower, or the *Gawain* poet. The latter's work contains many French as well as Scandinavian words, but then he was concerned to some extent to show that his understanding of courtly behaviour was, as a northern 'provincial' man, no less than that of southerners. In short, one must beware of making generalizations about 'the English language' on the basis of a sprinkling of surviving texts, since the relationship between what has survived and the over-all 'language' of the community which fostered it is not constant from one text to another nor from one generation to another. Even the extent to which a scribe was affected by the spelling conventions of the past, or of the text from which he was copying, varied from one man, or from one scriptorium, to another.

Shakespeare's language, and the language of the King James Bible, become steadily more remote from our own as does the literature of every past age. Literature is one of the conserving resources of a language, especially in an age when higher education is widespread; but in many cultures there has come a point where the language of the classical literature was so different from the language of everyday life that its study constituted the specialist occupation of a small *élite*. If the languages of such cultures also happen to have been used over a large geographical area and by many people – as has been the case for example with Chinese, with Latin, with Arabic (and with English) – the language of a literature may cease to bear any very close relationship to any of the spoken dialects; philology may then become a study of graphic forms, of the systems of an exclusively *written* code. The time may not be far off when English philology may have something of this meaning for scholars in, for example, India, Malaysia or Ceylon.

As a result of the historical sequence outlined at the beginning of this chapter, in the minds of some university teachers the study of literature became inseparable from philology. Philology itself being inseparable from the hard work of studying languages, it came to be thought that the study of literature would be too easy a discipline without such an element. There is, however, no doubt whatever that an interest in the structure and history of languages does not always coincide with an understanding of literature and the functions of criticism. There is no doubt also that a great deal of so-called 'philological' teaching in our universities in the past (and still in many continental universities today) has consisted of rather dreary textual and linguistic commentary of an uninformed kind, retained as a 'stiffener' to an equally uninformed literary study. As a result of this tendency some literary scholars reacted violently against all philology, and cast it out; to be branded as a philologist or a linguist or a 'language man' was to be excluded from polite society.

I believe this period to be passing. Younger generations of scholars recognize that the suspicions and hostilities of the past were misplaced. There are two discrete disciplines – the study of a language, and the study of a literature. Philology is, in its best relation to literature, the means by which the former illuminates the latter. But it is also the basis of much historical and comparative linguistics which has little immediate relation to the study of literature. Thus it is possible to make very valuable historical studies of the English language and of re-lated Germanic languages without considering the literary value of the texts used as evidence. Such studies are, however, seriously defective if they reveal (as unfortunately they so often have in the past) a lack of awareness that what is being dealt with is some aspect of the verbal behaviour of a particular society in a particular time and place; that behaviour, of course, includes the activities of the poets, the law-givers, the gram-marians, the merchants and the people in the streets and fields, churches and pubs.

Philology at its best must work not only within this general sociolinguistic framework of knowledge, but also within the framework of a general linguistic theory. We shall return to this point later.

## Dialectology and sociolinguistics

In addition to the recovery of texts and the historical study of the English language as revealed in them, there is a long tradi-tion in some English-speaking universities of the study of regional and social dialects and also of names (the latter being given sometimes the rather imposing title of Onomastics).

Dialect geography, the mapping of linguistic variation, had its origins curiously enough in the nineteenth-century theories about linguistic purity. The 'standard' form of a language (if one exists) tends to be based upon the dialect spoken in the capital or at court and to be given authority by the usage of writers and scholars and the activities of dictionary-makers and grammarians. The dialects of other regions, of less exalted social classes or less formal contexts tend to be relatively untouched by these activities, and to have no written form. But in a capital city people come together from all over the country and from abroad, and the urban dialect which is most closely related to the 'standard' often exhibits some of the features of a contact-variety – borrowed words, for example – and these tend to offend the purist especially if he finds corruption at court and matches that against the 'corruption' of the language. German scholars with antiquarian knowledge of older forms of German left the towns in the nineteenth century to search in rural areas for 'uncorrupted' forms of the language, 'the real old dialect'.

The myth about the 'purity' of an earlier stage of one's language has been widespread in history, paralleling similar myths about a golden age of man. The poet Spenser, reacting against what he considered to be the excessive use of Latinate and Italianate words by his contemporaries, looked back to Chaucer as 'a well of English undefiled', although in fact Chaucer's English was full of French. Linguists are not immune from such myths. A language is not a *thing*, that can be purified or contaminated, but a system of relationships between events which cannot be described except in terms of probabilities based on an analysis of past events. Our knowledge of past events is always imperfect, and there is always an element – usually considerable – of indeterminacy in our linguistic descriptions. The events are men's actions, their behaviour, symptomatic of their attempt to control their situation verbally. But most people are happier dealing with things. And so the dialectologists, going to the countryside to describe 'dialects', found themselves confronted with change and flux, but created 'things' by drawing static contours on the map.

The contours of linguistic atlases are known as isoglosses, by analogy with isobars and isotherms. They divide communities who use one linguistic feature from those who, instead, use a different one. For example, when vocabulary maps were drawn for the Linguistic Atlas of New England, one isogloss divided the regions where informants had used *spigot* from those where they had used *faucet* for a water-tap; when pronunciation is investigated for England, we can map those areas in which people use a burred 'r' in words like *bird*, or those in which people use the northern, front 'a' in *glass* rather than the

southern, back 'a'; or where people say *greasy* with a voiceless
's' rather than a voiced 'z', or where they have no clear pre-
ference. Morphological, syntactic and semantic features can be
mapped in a similar fashion, and for a number of years now
such dialect mapping has been going on in various parts of the
English-speaking world, as well as for other language-communities. The various isoglosses rarely coincide with one
another; a language-community is found to be a *continuum*,
but thick bundles of isoglosses – which often coincide with
geographical features such as rivers, mountain-barriers, forests
or a major route which people travel along but rarely cross –
tell us something about the location of communities within the
wider community.

The English Place-Names Society had its data already to a
large extent recorded for it – the names of places, rivers, fords,
hills and valleys in early documents. The Society has published
extensive studies of the elements found in each name and the
etymology of these elements. Such work goes hand-in-hand
with archaeology in illuminating the history of Britain through
the traces left by each wave of colonists in their names. It need
not be confined to the early history – the Britons, Romans,
Anglo-Saxons, Vikings and Normans; a study of street-names
and of the words used for 'street' or 'road' in different parts of
any large town will reveal something about the settlement
history of the town and the fashions of each age, right down
to the present day.

The framework of sociolinguistics has given new dimensions
and a new coherence to the study of dialects. Previously, studies
have been based to a large extent on selecting an informant
and using him to represent the village or parish. The antiquarian and folk-lore element in such collecting has remained
strong (as a perusal of any issue of the *Bulletin of the Yorkshire
Dialect Society* or of *American Speech* will show), and the
informant has tended to be one of the oldest and least-travelled
members of the community. This has had the advantage of
preserving an element of comparability from parish to parish,
but it reflects a somewhat static and 'golden age' view of
society. In any society there are social as well as geographical
isoglosses, and social and geographical mobility. The work
planned for the Tyneside Linguistic Survey (directed from

Newcastle University) and that carried out, for example, by William Labov in New York, both illustrate the contrast between sociolinguistics and dialect geography – although the latter forms part of the former. Labov made use of a socio-economic survey of the Lower East Side of New York City to investigate the verbal behaviour of a sample of the same people. He used the same class divisions – defined by income and level of education – of lower working class, working class, middle class, upper middle class and upper class, and took samples of his informants' speech in less formal and more formal contexts. From these he extracted information about the incidence of post-vocalic 'r' (for example, in phrases such as *fourth floor*) and four other features of pronunciation, and he found that when placed in a more formal situation each class adjusted its usage so as to be more like that of the class above. Other studies along somewhat similar lines are being made in the West Indies and in Africa. Language – specifically the English language – is thus being treated as a significant variable in the behaviour of social groups; a language or a dialect is viewed, not as a homogeneous or static 'thing', but as an abstraction from states of change and systematic diversity. I will return to this point when discussing general linguistics.

Major surveys are under way today of various registers and styles of use within the English language community – for example, the intensive study of educated southern British usage at University College, London – or of the social and cultural significance of diversity in usage, as in the Tyneside Survey already mentioned, or in the survey of Creole English being carried out by the Language Department at York. Such work involves the anthropologist, the linguist, the sociologist, the psychologist and the statistician; it is in its infancy, but can perhaps provide considerable insight into the behaviour of individuals and of communities as revealed through their linguistic systems. It is of prime importance in trying to understand and assess the direction and motivation of cultural changes in multilingual communities. In many of these – for example, in the developing countries of the Commonwealth, in New York or Georgia, in Ireland, in Quebec, in immigrant centres in Great Britain – English is one of the languages concerned; and the tensions between Anglo-Saxon cultural attributes and those of another society trying to form, or feeling itself culturally threatened or economically frustrated, are the source of difficult social problems in which the student and teacher of the English language finds himself involved. One's linguistic behaviour is a series of acts of identity; and many communities are identified, both by their members and by others, more by their language than by other means.

The combination of studies required for sociolinguistics is more common at present in the United States than in Britain, but it is slowly making headway in this country.

## Historical studies of English dialects

The dialect studies so far referred to have been synchronic – that is, taking a cross-section of the language in use at a particular point in time. Historical philology has been described in so far as generalizations are made for 'the English language' as a whole. But in addition, there has at some universities for a long time been a strong tradition of the historical study of various English dialects, and of their changing relationship to the standard language (or, more correctly, of the standard language to the dialects).

In any country, linguistic diversity reflects the patterns of migration and contact – contact with other communities is the chief reason for linguistic change, and the most conservative communities are those which are most isolated from contact. In England our regional dialects originally reflected: first, the regions in which different waves of migration from continental Europe landed; second, the subsequent contact of the migrants and their settler-descendants, both with the indigenous British and with the traders and further colonizers who came from the continent; third, the degree of mobility – geographical and social – within each region and between one region and another; fourth, the standard and nature and extent of literacy in any particular community – ranging from literacy in Latin for a tiny *élite* to mass literacy in the vernacular; fifth, arising out of literacy, the accidents of history which have ordained that a major poet or writer should be born into a particular community to use the language of that community and help to give it prestige, as Dante did for Tuscan and Chaucer for London

English; sixth, the accidents of both geography and history which led to the capital and cultural centres being established – at Lindisfarne, Winchester, York, London or Canterbury, for example.

Within the field of historical dialect studies there have again been those who took a comparatively static and those who took a more or less dynamic approach. The first have tended to assume historical continuity over many generations of the same families, the same culture in the same place; the latter have recognized to a greater or less extent that such assumptions, though convenient, do not always stand up to detailed probing; that people and populations move, that cultures and kingdoms rise and fall, trade patterns, education systems and the whole social fabric can change. Who today lives in the same part of the country as both his grandfathers? In what sense can we speak of continuity in the Northumbrian or Anglian dialect when the eastern part of England was overrun again and again in the ninth, tenth and eleventh centuries by Vikings? We can compare texts written in Northumbria in A.D. 800 with texts written in Northumbria in 1000, but whether we can make very meaningful statements in such terms as 'the Northumbrian dialect changed from x to y' will depend upon our awareness of the relationship between the texts, the population from which they came and the linguistic abstractions we are making on the basis of the texts.

Today there is an increased awareness that the historical study of English dialects must include those that have spread overseas, and that the processes we can observe at work overseas may help to explain what has happened in Britain in the past. There still remains to be written a colonization history of the English language, but contributory studies are going on in many parts of the world. Such work helps greatly to illuminate historical linguistics generally; moreover it is likely that historical linguistics, and historical dialectology in particular, will undergo major changes of perspective in the next few years as synchronic and diachronic studies re-converge.

## Contact and Creole varieties of English

One of the most potent disciplines in bringing these two

G

approaches – the synchronic and diachronic (or historical) –
together again after their long divorce has been the study of
Creole languages. Creoles and creolized varieties of English
are spoken in many parts of the world: in the Sea Islands off
the Carolina coast, in the West Indies and around the coasts
of Central America, in Surinam and Guyana, in West, Central
and East Africa, in Melanesia and elsewhere. They have been
studied more or less systematically since Schuchardt began
publishing his *Kreolische Studien* in the latter part of the nineteenth century; the phenomena which they illustrate in an
accentuated form are general linguistic phenomena, and so the
study of Creole English (called Pidgin English in some parts of
the world, although linguists only speak of a pidgin as long as
it is nobody's native language) highlights these and helps to
make one reconsider all the linguistic generalizations made on
the basis of studying the languages of more stable, longer-
established, more homogeneous communities. Here is language
in the making; it arrests our attention because it is called
English but we do not understand it; we learn to understand
it, and the processes of producing it, and we then find that we
are understanding far better what happens generally in communities to produce 'a language' – that language is in the
making every day and everywhere, and that the study of the
processes involved is a lens for the study of man through his
most essentially human activity. The consequent approach to
English language studies, which brings together the Yorkshireman, the Indian, the Australian, the Pakistani, the Nigerian
and the Londoner to study one another, has the incidental
result of being very destructive of communal prejudice.

**Etymology, lexicography and semantics**

The study of the derivations and meanings of words is one of
the most popular and appealing branches of language study;
it provides scope for the amateur in popular journalism, and in
local dialect collecting, as well as for the very scholarly activities
of the editors of the *Oxford English Dictionary* and the
*Dictionary of American Regional English*. A new supplement to
the thirteen volumes of the former is being prepared at Oxford;
the original ten volumes (of the *New English Dictionary*) took

from 1884 until 1928 to complete. The *Dictionary of American Regional English* is under preparation at the University of Wisconsin and should be complete within about ten years. There are other regional and historical dictionaries of English either already published or in preparation: the *English Dialect Dictionary* which a Yorkshireman, Joseph Wright, published at his own expense with the Clarendon Press at the beginning of this century; the *Dictionary of American English*; *Dictionary of Jamaican English*; *Dictionary of Canadianisms*; *Dictionary of the Older Scottish Tongue*; *Scottish National Dictionary*; *Anglo-Saxon Dictionary*; *Middle English Dictionary*; not to mention *Webster's International Dictionary* and the various specialized dictionaries compiled by enthusiasts such as Eric Partridge, or the *Dictionary of Mining Terms, Dictionary of Herbs* and a hundred others. In most of the first group the method employed owes a great deal to Dr Samuel Johnson, whose dictionary originally appeared in two volumes in 1755. Citations are collected – either wholly from literature or partly from spoken records – and grouped so as to establish the morphological and semantic developments of words from one generation to the next. Meanings are defined partly by synonyms, partly by citing the actual contexts in which the word has been recorded. The editor must decide, by establishing morphological and form-class criteria, how to arrange his entries: whether, for example, to cure a patient and to cure tobacco are two examples of the same, or examples of two different, words; and, by establishing etymological criteria, in what sense one word can be said to derive from another, or be related to another. If he is compiling a specialized dictionary – for example, a *Dictionary of Australian English* – he must establish criteria of usage to decide what constitutes an item in Australian as contrasted with American or British or Jamaican English: it may be that the word was first recorded in Australia, or in a book about Australia, or in a sense only applicable in Australia; or that it has survived in use in Australia after it has passed out of use elsewhere, and so on.

Lexicographers of English today face difficult problems which did not loom very large for Dr Johnson. These are partly due to the world-wide extension of English, and partly to the changes which have affected linguistic theory in the past fifty years. It is no longer possible to describe any variety of English in terminology which implies homogeneity. We may begin by describing the *idiolect* of a particular individual, all the patterns of behaviour which allow us to predict the probability of usage of that individual in any particular context; we can pass on to do the same for other similarly-educated members of the same community, and we can then make an abstraction which we can call a description of the dialect of that community, although it will only hold true for any particular member to a limited extent. If we then do the same for other communities we may end by abstracting from these dialect descriptions those features which they all have in common, or we may attempt to make a catholic and comprehensive statement which again will only hold true for each community to a limited extent – and we may claim that either of these is a statement about 'the English language'. It must be clear that the more numerous and the more widespread a language community may be, the less any particular statement about that 'language' is likely to be true for any individual member. Thus the student of lexicography must always ask, what does a dictionary represent? Is it a record of every word that has ever been used by any member of the community? If so, many archaisms, unassimilated loans, nonce-usages and malapropisms would have to be included. Do the words have to have been recorded in the written literature? If so, a great many non-literary dialects of great interest would be excluded. To what extent are historical and geographical variation in form, meaning, or functional load and distribution to be recorded? It is quite wrong to suppose that 'a language' necessarily has 'more words in it' because it possesses a bigger dictionary; the average speaker of English is only familiar with a very small proportion of the words recorded in *The Oxford English Dictionary*.

The mode of arrangement of the material within a dictionary is also of interest, and provides problems for the compiler. It may be compiled as an alphabetical index. It may be that derivation will be allowed for in the compilation, so that *lace-work* will come under *lace* and precede *lacerate*. It may be that some elements of a thesaurus are to be included, so that the reader can be referred to a range of morphemes in the same semantic field; it may be that the dictionary is intended to be encyclopaedic, giving far more information about a word than the citations of usage commonly give. The lexicographer, like all other descriptive scientists, must in the end take the responsibility for the patterns he imposes upon his material. The suffix – *ish*, for example, is very productive in English, and its meanings range through those in *Danish, heathenish, boyish, womanish, dampish, selfish, sevenish, Jewish, goatish, bookish* and *feverish*. The lexicographer must decide to some extent arbitrarily whether he wishes to treat all of these under one, two, three or more headings. He will very frequently ponder the questions, 'what do we mean by a word?' 'in what sense is this word the same as that word?', and 'what do we mean by the meaning of a word?'

General studies of the English lexicon show that great changes have taken place since Anglo-Saxon times, and these are of interest both from the point of view of semantic theory and sociologically. Each fresh cultural contact – through the penetration of Great Britain by missionaries or colonizers or immigrants, through the travels and colonization of English-speaking people overseas, or simply through the arrival of new ideas – has added new lexical items to the vocabulary and modified in some way the form and meaning of existing items. Changes within English society, brought about for example by the introduction of printing, the progressive spread of education and increasing social and geographical mobility, have led to an increasing degree of standardization in the forms and meanings of the lexicon.

We can therefore study the lexicon from a number of different points of view, to try to answer some of the following questions: What was the nature and extent of the lexicon available to any particular person, or any particular community, at any particular time? What does the study of this lexicon tell us about the environment and culture of that person or community? What differences can we describe between one such lexicon and another? What can the study of such differences tell us about changes in environment or culture? What does a consideration of the lexicon tell us about 'meaning' in general, or about the meaning of particular items? How does 'change of meaning' come about? In what sense can we recapture the meanings of a former age, or learn the meanings of another community, or even of another person? Such questions lead us inevitably to a consideration of the nature of 'meaning', a consideration equally vital to philosophers, to students of poetry, to linguists and to all who engage in argument or rhetoric. It is not possible even to embark upon the discussion here, beyond saying that the primary connection between a word and its 'meaning' is that the word was uttered by a particular person in a particular context at a particular time, and perhaps heard by others with particular results. This consideration is more important and more basic than the notion of 'reference' or 'denotation' from which much discussion of meaning starts. It may be that the child learning his language takes a great leap forward when he grasps the notion that 'things' can be 'pointed to' with 'names'; but such an experience only covers a very limited part of his total linguistic knowledge. He will develop for himself a meaning for the word 'true' out of the circumstances in which he encounters the word. A word is an event, and meaning is a relationship between events. Reference is a secondary property more apparent for some words than for others. Seen in this way, poetic meaning is essentially no different from everyday meaning.

## Descriptive studies of modern English in the light of general linguistics, psychology and sociology

### Phonetics; speaking and hearing in relation to language-learning

In Europe, phonetics is one of the oldest branches of descriptive linguistics, and some of the outstanding writers on the subject have been concerned with English pronunciation. The so-called orthoepists from the sixteenth century onwards – some of them appalled by the rate at which English pronunciation was changing and getting out of step with English spelling – wrote handbooks advising those in need of help how to pronounce English so as to pass in polite society.

In Bernard Shaw's play *Pygmalion* Professor Henry Higgins undertook that Eliza Doolittle should achieve the same end – to pass for a lady by changing her vowels. The original of Henry Higgins was Henry Sweet, after many vicissitudes and rebuffs Reader in Phonetics at Oxford at the end of the nineteenth century, who is generally considered to be the founder of modern phonetics. An ancillary stream of activity has been the devising of shorthand systems for the rapid transcription of speech. Sweet himself owed some of his inspiration to A. Melville Bell's *Visible Speech*, published in 1863. Sweet in 1885 published in German an elementary handbook of spoken English, through which he made familiar to continental students his methods of describing the sounds of a language. He was outstanding as a phonetician, as an historian of the English language, as an editor of early English texts, as a general philologist and linguist and as a trainer of language-teachers. His successors, in Europe, England and America, have frequently been concerned with language teaching; they have nearly all been practical men, and laboratory scientists. Many of them have been missionaries concerned with describing and teaching hitherto unrecorded languages.

The language teacher is concerned to get his pupils to articulate the speech-sounds of a language, and he tries to describe those sounds in articulatory terms – that is, to say how they are made, what physical organs are involved and in what manner. The shorthand-writer, on the other hand, is concerned with recapturing the auditory impression made on him. In the last half-century the development of instruments such as the kymograph, the microphone, the oscillograph, the sonograph and the oscillomink have made it possible to measure and describe both the sound-waves of speech and the movements of air which accompany these. Acoustic phonetics has made enormous strides; the title of A. Melville Bell's *Visible Speech* was used again for the publication in 1947 of the work of scientists at the Bell Telephone Laboratories in America which led to the sound spectrograph, a machine which traces the amplitude and duration of the components of speech-sounds over a great range of frequencies so as to present a shaded graph, or picture, of those components and to lead on to the speech-synthesizer. This machine, being given data of the kind produced by the sound spectrograph, will reproduce speech sounds. A further practical application of the 'pictures' produced by the sound spectrograph has been in teaching deaf children to speak, since they can be trained to reproduce on an oscillograph screen through trial and error of speech the 'picture' they see on the spectrograph trace. Spectrographic analysis has led also to certain discoveries about the fundamental nature of speech-sounds; and it has the great virtue of allowing the analysis of continuous speech instead of speech-sounds uttered in isolation. It is fair to say that the tape-recorder and the sound-spectrograph have between them revolutionized acoustic phonetics.

Articulatory phonetics has always practised a certain degree of sleight-of-hand (or ear). In the first place, the manner of segmentation of speech into discrete 'speech-sounds' owes, in its origin, something to the alphabetic nature of our writing system. This has had a bias towards morphophonemic rather than phonetic representation and in its origins selected for representation those features which made significant differences between one word and another in Semitic and Indo-European languages, rather than the universals of speech-sounds. The work of the International Phonetic Association and of modern phoneticians in general has striven to adapt phonetic writing so as to give a more fundamental analysis of articulation, but the alphabetic bias remains.

In the second place, statements as to how speech-sounds are made depend upon physiological observation. A great deal of this has been done in the laboratory. X-ray photographs have been taken to determine the position of the tongue when pronouncing different vowel-sounds; small mirrors and cameras can be introduced into the vocal organs to help with observation, and so on. It is not very difficult to observe the operation of the lips, to feel whether or not aspiration is taking place, or whether or not the vocal chords are vibrating at any particular moment. Nevertheless, much elementary training in phonetics consists of being taught to identify *acoustic data* with *articulatory specifications* which have to be taken on trust by the student; and anybody who has watched a good ventriloquist knows that there must be more than one way of creating certain auditory impressions. The evidence provided by the acoustic analyses of the sound spectograph has been a challenge to articulatory phonetics to re-examine and refine its procedures.

The study of the neural mechanisms whereby the articulatory processes are set in motion has not until recently impinged much upon linguistics, although the remedial work of the speech-therapist with stammerers involves a knowledge of articulatory phonetics. There have been a great many studies of pathological conditions such as aphasia, in which neural or memory defects inhibit speech, but few of the normal neural processes. Today however the study of both speaking and hearing processes are bringing together a number of disciplines including linguistics.

## Hearing

Language implies not only a speaker but a hearer, but less work had been done until recently on the manner in which we hear speech-sounds than on the manner in which we make them. Not only are the auditory mechanisms of the ear, of other parts of the bone and tissue structure of the head, of the neural circuits to the brain, involved, but also the mental processes of perception, the study of which is usually undertaken by the experimental psychologist and the neuro-physiologist.

Such studies are again of importance to the language-teacher, since we perceive things by matching our sense-impressions against the perceptual systems we have already created. Stimuli of light and shade, and of different wave-lengths of light, are interpreted in terms of a street, houses, people. Similarly, stimuli consisting of noises are interpreted in terms of speech-sounds, words and sentences. The perceptual system which we use to analyse new verbal experiences will be based on the linguistic system we have created to date. Much of the noise will be ignored as irrelevant, as 'noise' rather than 'signal', and 'signals' will be interpreted as far as possible in terms of the distinctive features of our own language. Thus, in the general field of second-language learning, and among the very large number of people concerned today with teaching English to those for whom it is not a native language, the studies of 'interference' between linguistic systems and of the motivation for language choice in multilingual situations are of great importance.

The role of the psychologist is evident when we study hearing and perception; evident also when we study learning, both how children and adults learn a language, and also the *rôle* of language in learning generally. It has in the past been less evident, but is coming to assume greater importance, when we study how it is that people can speak a language; how can one produce every day hundreds of utterances, the majority of which have never been uttered or heard or read before, confident that there is a high probability that the person to whom we are speaking will recognize them and respond appropriately?

To answer this question has been one of the central concerns of the generative grammarians who have come into prominence within the past decade. Their grammars are called 'generative' because they are concerned to set out series of 'rules', the 'knowledge' of which will enable the user of the language to generate and to understand new 'sentences'. (The precise significance of each of the words in inverted commas is in dispute!) But in order to see their achievements (and their quarrels) in perspective it is necessary to consider, however briefly, the whole relationship between developments in this century in general linguistics and the study of the English language.

## General linguistic theory and the study of the English language

My remarks so far have, in a number of places, raised questions about the theoretical framework within which the English language is to be studied. Many generations of scholars have in the past studied 'the English language' by reading texts and pursuing activities of a philological kind, without asking such questions as: what is the relationship in general of written language to spoken language? Is this constant for all societies? What is the nature of the construct we refer to as 'the language', or of 'language' in general? Exactly how is language transmitted, from one generation to another, or from one community to another? If we are asked to describe 'a language', what should we take as our raw material, along what dimensions should we investigate its variations, what form should our description take? In what sense can we then 'relate' one such 'language' to another? Does the term 'the English language' have linguistic, or only psychological and sociological, significance? How, for example, does it differ from 'the American language'? In what sense do we still speak 'the same language' as Chaucer? (How do the 'German' dialects on one side of the frontier with Holland differ from the closely-similar 'Dutch' dialects on the other side? Is it simply because people on one side *think* they are speaking 'German', and, on the other side, 'Dutch'?) Is language a peculiar property of the human species? Are there any universal laws which govern its nature? In what sense and to what extent are all human languages governed by these laws? Is it possible to seal off 'language' from other kinds of human behaviour, and write rules which will have predictive value for a language without reference to the context or to other behavioural systems? What is the relationship between a language and the environment in which it is used? Do the lexical and grammatical differences between old and modern English betray real differences of outlook, as literary critics constantly interpret them to do? And so on . . .

Increasingly, and rightly, it is becoming necessary to have at least some acquaintance with the investigation of such questions if one is to be seriously regarded as a student of the English language. There have of course been many philosophers and linguists in the past concerned with such questions, although there has tended to be an unfortunate divorce between the approach of the speculative philosophers and that of the linguists. Our knowledge of philosopher-linguists goes back to the fifth century B.C. in Greece and in India; to Plato, and to the forerunners of Pāṇini. In the present century we have seen philosophers such as Wittgenstein and Ryle become increasingly preoccupied with the nature of language, and linguists such as De Saussure, Jespersen, Sapir, Hjelmslev, Bloomfield and Chomsky approaching from very varied kinds of investigation the same central questions. Today the philosopher, the psychologist, the anthropologist, the sociologist and the neuro-physiologist are forced increasingly to look at the structure of linguistic data for clues, and the linguist in turn looks to these other disciplines for help. Coincidentally English has become the most widely-used language in the world (although Chinese is used by more people); its structure is tested in response to the greatest variety of situations, and it is the most commonly used international language of scholars. Theories about language are more likely to be worked out in

English, and transmitted to other scholars in English, than in any other language. This situation carries great dangers, since it may be that the structure of very-widely spoken languages such as English and Chinese is quite different in important respects from that of the languages of small homogeneous and non-literate groups, but that unless we can study languages of very different kinds we will mistake our statements about English for universally-valid rules. On the other hand, since most of the work in linguistics has been done within the Indo-European tradition it may be that we are already, in trying to analyse English and Chinese, prisoners of the past, inhibited by the generalizations we have long been taught to make about Latin and Greek and Sanskrit. One of the central difficulties about linguistics as a science is that the meta-language we use to discuss our language is virtually the same as the language we are discussing; it is very easy, when searching for linguistic universals, unwittingly to impose them upon the data because they are already implicit in the semantic structure of the meta-language. If we say 'let us see if all languages have nouns', then we have already imposed upon language a universal category, the noun. It is rather like saying, 'let us see if all fish can swim', when implicit in our definition of a fish is the fact that it lives in water, and implicit in the meaning of 'swim' is the sense, *to move in water*.

Since this chapter is concerned specifically with the study of the English language it would not be right to spend too much time on the current controversies within general linguistics. It is sufficient to say that they are highly stimulating, and not easy to generalize about. It is significant that many of the leading controversialists have felt that they must write their own 'introductions' to linguistics, to describe the foundations upon which they wish to build. During the second quarter of the present century great progress was made in refining the methods used for describing languages, particularly by anthropologists and missionaries; this progress came first in phonetics, then in phonology and then in morphology; there was however little comparable progress in syntax, and virtually none in semantic theory. In a highly-inflected language the syntactic relationship between the parts of an utterance are very often marked by some inflexional suffix, so that the section of the grammar called 'morphology' or 'accidence' is a major part of the whole; such markers not only indicate, e.g. 'this adjective modifies that noun and both form the subject, or object, of the sentence' but they also indicate the *boundaries* of the subject, or the object, or the verb, phrase. English is not a highly-inflected language, and Chinese is not inflected at all; these boundaries are often therefore lacking. When English utterances are put in their written form (which does not reveal their stress and intonation patterns) and quoted out of context, therefore, there tends often to be some apparent ambiguity as to their syntactic structure which is only resolved by our know-ledge of the semantic probabilities. This apparent syntactic ambiguity has long been exploited by poets; it has also been the starting-point for a major new onslaught on certain aspects of syntax by Noam Chomsky and other transformational-generative grammarians, who feel that ambiguous construc-tions, pairs of sentences whose surface-structure is apparently the same or similar, can be elucidated by tracing their origin in underlying structures which differ from each other.

In a non-inflecting language, however, such clarification must often depend upon semantic understanding. For example, a sentence which may be written as

It made her a marvellous pet.

can be interpreted either in the sense that something happened to turn *her* into a marvellous pet for somebody, or in the sense that something became a marvellous pet to give to *her*. There will possibly be differences of stress and intonation between these two when spoken, but these may be idiosyncratic. My own feeling is that *made* will possibly be more heavily stressed in the first sense than in the second. If, however, we replace *pet* by *mother* the possibility of two interpretations is reduced very considerably, since we know that *mother* is more likely to relate back to *her* than to *it*. We can rewrite the first sentence in two ways which mark the underlying structure more clearly, by transforming it into two different passive constructions:

(1) *She* was turned into a marvellous pet.
(2) It was turned into a marvellous pet for *her*.

The *rôle* of the female in question is now marked as that of the subject in the first sentence, and so contrasted with her *rôle* in the second as a qualifier of the objective *a marvellous pet*.

To a certain extent we can handle such problems in English by what are conventionally regarded as syntactic means – the arrangement of word-classes in order and the way in which they are 'clustered' by various marking devices; to a certain extent we need semantic knowledge in order to say to which word-class English words unmarked by their form belong. For example, in the (often-quoted) set of sentences

    (1) She made him a good husband.
    (2) She made him a good partner.
    (3) She made him a good wife.
    (4) She made him a good dinner.
    (5) She made him a good deal worse.

there is little chance of alternative interpretations of either (1) or (3) because we know that *husband* belongs to a class habitually also referred to by *him*, and *wife* to a class habitually referred to by *she*. Most people tend to think of *partner* as more likely to be male than female, but it could be either; and most people tend to think of *dinner* as neither although in fact – were *she* in one case or *he* in the other a cannibal – it could be either. In (5) we need to know the whole idiom, *a good deal worse*. And so the possibilities of variant interpretations are reduced in various ways – by our semantic understanding, and by our knowledge of the probabilities. Irony would allow us to refer to a woman making a good husband by being the dominant partner, but this would not be the first 'sentence' we would reconstruct from the written clues. *She made him a good husband* and the other examples are not in fact English sentences but rather sets of black marks on white paper arranged in conventional ways so as to give clues to the reader from which he can construct for himself English sentences. It may be that in some cases of 'ambiguity' discussed at length by the grammarians the problem is simply that not enough clues have been given.

It is the aim of the transformational-generative grammarians to discover among the underlying structures of sentences logical universals of syntax which apply in any language. It has even been suggested that some 'knowledge' of such universals is innate, and may be related to the structure of the human brain. It may be that present lines of enquiry will lead only to such 'universals' of behaviour as fear, doubt, desire and the need for expressive affirmation; that the borderline between syntax – about which we are beginning to understand a little – and semantics, about which we understand very little indeed, does not lie in the same place for all languages, nor even perhaps for all members of the same language-community; that some grammatical devices originate in mnemonic and deictic functions which do not operate in a written code in the same way as in speech, and that the 'language' of a highly-literate community is in some ways a different animal from that of a non-literate community. It may be that the learning-processes with which we are concerned are not language-specific, and that the logic of human behaviour, of which language is a part, is infinitely more complex even than the perplexing problems so far handled by grammarians. Nevertheless, there is a great deal of excitement in the quest; many alternative generative hypotheses to transformational grammar are being proposed and tested – in America, in Europe and in Britain; and the study of the English language within this framework suggests the possibility of great gains in psychological insight.

## Style and stylistics

A discussion of syntax and lexicon leads on naturally to the problem of style, since variations of style can be defined in terms of syntactic and lexical choice or, as one writer put it, 'putting the right words in the right places'. The two choices are always interdependent, not independent. Stylistics is one of the most ill-defined and ill-explored of subjects, a no-man's-land between linguistics and literary criticism. Intimate acquaintance with the utterances of a particular person or period helps us to identify new examples, and there have been many attempts in the past to analyse and quantify the cues by which we carry out these acts of recognition. Confident statements have been made on the basis of such quantification, for example as to the authorship of 'Shakespearian' plays or of the Pauline epistles. Certain linguistic features are very easy to count: average sentence-length, the comparative incidence of inversion of the most normal subject-verb-object order, the incidence of co-ordinating constructions as compared with subordinating, and so on. Lexical items of little semantic significance may be important stylistically – a fondness for *furthermore* rather than *further*, for example; lexical items of greater significance are less easy to count in any meaningful way in comparable samples because their use depends on the subject under discussion. One can sometimes, in a language like English, which offers hosts of near-synonyms, distinguish a consistently 'learned' style using Latinate terms from a more 'popular' one using more words of Anglo-Saxon origin.

An interesting study was made in 1967 for the Office of Scientific and Technical Information (R. Huddleston *et al.*, *Sentence and Clause in Scientific English*) of the syntax of 'scientific English' at three levels: that of the learned and specialist journal, that of the not-quite-so specialist, and that of the popularizing journal; the authors have made use of M. A. K. Halliday's 'scale-and-category' model of syntactic analysis for identifying and counting syntactic features, and the tables they present enable us to make certain generalizations about these three levels of presentation. To a certain extent each of us, when writing scientific English, will be under pressure to conform to one of these registers, just as the aspiring journalist may feel he has to write like *Time* magazine; but the possibilities of making a stylish choice occur at so many different points in a sentence or a paragraph that style ulti-mately belongs to the idiosyncratic end of the linguistic spectrum, and the things which the linguist can say about it, although interesting, are relatively crude. Moreover, many of the cues derive from the lucidity or power of a man's thought rather than from quantifiable aspects of his linguistic usage. There is in the last resort no substitute for reading with critical attention as much as possible of the work of a particular writer or period; all that the linguist can do is to help with the training of that critical attention. This is itself, however, quite an important *rôle*.

## Conclusion

In writing this chapter I have set the study of the English language within the framework of general linguistics as a behavioural science. It is only fair to say that many philologists and linguists would find such an approach uncongenial; they would feel that their studies should be confined to the properties of the formal systems inherent in or abstracted from linguistic data. There is no contradiction between the two approaches, but if *explanations* are sought for linguistic behaviour rather than, simply, *descriptions*, then the explanations cannot be found wholly within the description of the linguistic systems however detailed or 'deep' these may be; they will be found partly in the social or psychological circumstances to which the language is a response.

## Suggested reading

I am indebted to Alan S. C. and Stefanyja Ross for reading this chapter and correcting many of my mistakes. Those that remain are due to my obstinacy.

Three very good and easily-accessible books relating to the topics in this chapter are:

A. C. Gimson, *An Introduction to the Pronunciation of English*, second ed., Edward Arnold, 1970.

John Lyons, *Introduction to Theoretical Linguistics*, Cambridge University Press, 1968.

Randolph Quirk, *Essays on the English Language Medieval and Modern*, Longmans, 1968.

For a straightforward if somewhat old-fashioned historical account readers should refer to Albert C. Baugh, *A History of the English Language*, Routledge & Kegan Paul, 2nd ed., 1959.

For a good, eclectic account of modern theoretical work, see H. A. Gleason, *Linguistics and English Grammar*, New York: Holt, Rinehart, 1965.

A number of papers relating to transformational-generative theory and English language studies have recently been brought together in David A. Reibel and Sanford A. Schane (eds.), *Modern Studies in English*, Englewood Cliffs, N.J.: Prentice-Hall, 1969.

Those interested in various aspects of a more behavioural approach will find stimulus and reward in:

Roger Brown, *Words and Things*, London: Collier-Macmillan, 1958.

Roger Brown, *Social Psychology*, London: Collier-Macmillan, 1965.

Peter Herriot, *An Introduction to the Psychology of Language*, Methuen, 1970.

R. C. Oldfield and J. C. Marshall (eds.), *Language*, Penguin Books, 1968.

L. S. Vygotsky, *Thought and Language* (translated by E. Haufmann and G. Vakar), Cambridge, Mass.: MIT Press, 1962.

In the field of semantics, see Geoffrey N. Leech, *Towards a Semantic Description of English*, Longmans, 1969.

For a sample of Creole English studies, see:

Beryl Loftman Bailey, *Creole English Syntax*, Cambridge University Press, 1966.

F. G. Cassidy and R. B. Le Page, *Dictionary of Jamaican English*, Cambridge University Press, 1967.

# 6

# Literature in English in Overseas Societies

*Gerald Moore*

The recognition of English as a major vehicle of creative expression in overseas societies has been a phenomenon of the past twenty-five years. The recognition has trailed somewhat behind the facts, but it would be true to say that, outside the United States, there was relatively little work of quality before 1945 on which serious literary studies could be based. Even such long-established English-speaking communities as those of Canada, South Africa, Australia and New Zealand had done little to establish their claims upon the literary attention of the world. A few names – Katherine Mansfield, Olive Schreiner, Roy Campbell, William Plomer – had emerged from the prevailing atmosphere of provincialism and mediocrity which was felt to surround 'the colonies'.

In recent years voices full of authority, urgency and eloquence have floated to us, not only from the major areas of white settlement, but from areas which few English people associated with the confident, creative handling of 'our' language; from Africa, from the West Indies, from India and even further afield. What happens when a black man who knows us only through our literature and who feels that literature speaks only in part to his condition, confronts the language with the full rush of his own living?

Let us begin with the passionate irony of Derek Walcott, the black West Indian poet who has helped as much as anyone to establish the claims of overseas writing in English to our attention. In a recent poem called 'Crusoe's Journal', Walcott

turns the story of Crusoe and Friday into a parable of the
cultural deprivation of his own people, torn loose from Africa
centuries ago and left stranded on a string of little islands where
even the demands of European commerce no longer require
their slavery, or even their presence. Having lost so much of
their own heritage in language, custom and a familiar past,
their colonial education asks them to take as substitutes the
language and civilization of those who first enslaved and then
abandoned them. Walcott writes as a 'castaway' thrown up by
chance and history on an empty strand:[1]

> out of such timbers
> came our first book, our profane Genesis
>     whose Adam speaks that prose
> which, blessing some sea-rock, startles itself
>     with poetry's surprise
> in a green world, one without metaphors;
>     like Christofer he bears
> in speech mnemonic as a missionary's
>     the Word to savages,
> its shape an earthen, water-bearing vessel's
>     whose sprinkling alters us
> into good Fridays who recite his praise,
>     parroting our master's
> style and voice, we make his language ours,
>     converted cannibals
> we learn with him to eat the flesh of Christ.

Walcott's method here is to seduce us initially by the familiar
*appearance* of his poem, only to administer a delayed shock as
we receive the import of his irony. His poetry handles the
apparatus of 'Eng. Lit.', its prosody, its patterns of reference
and allusion, to release the hard energy of an individual style
which reminds us in every line that his race, climate, landscape
and historical experience are not ours. This is a far cry from
the 'parroting' of which he mockingly accuses himself.

If Walcott sees himself as a kind of flotsam stranded on the
white beaches of the Caribbean, then the sea-worn words of
our language are a jetsam washed up beside him. Out of the
bitter struggle to survive in an environment unfamiliar to them
both, may come a new literature, a new language and a new

people. For Caribbean English, which has been shaped for centuries by the speech and song of the folk, will now be shaped by its writers also into a language discernibly different from that of its original home in the North.

To put this development in perspective, we must remember that the native speakers of English (including its many dialects) now form a world-wide army in which the people of Britain itself are only a small and territorially restricted regiment. In North America alone, the native speakers of our tongue out-number us by nearly five to one. Add to this nearly five millions, of predominantly African extraction, but with sub-stantial infusions of Indian and Chinese blood, in the Carib-bean islands and on the mainland of South and Central America. Add again the twenty millions of Australia and New Zealand; the settled English-speaking populations of Central and Southern Africa and those mixed communities, held together only by the language and their physical isolation, in places such as St Helena, Tristan da Cunha, the Seychelles, the Falk-lands, Pitcairn Island and Gibraltar. To all these millions of people, scattered over every continent, the very act of writing almost dictates the choice of English. Hence the study of English and its attendant literatures, in British universities, should open windows for us, not only upon our own culture, but upon the world outside.

As we have seen, however, the flow of literature which is today enriching the common stream of English expression does not stem only from those areas where it has become the native tongue. Equally significant in the development of English as a creative medium has been its rapid growth in many parts of Africa and Asia. As with the Roman Empire long ago, the language has not departed with the last imperial legions. Indeed, the rapid spread of education in Africa since indepen-dence means that there are now far more people involved in handling English there than ever before. No longer is it simply a *lingua franca* for the *élite*, but the major medium of higher education, government, debate and journalism, touching very large areas of the population. To a surprising extent, the same is true of India and Pakistan, and of such great international centres as Singapore and Hong Kong. It is no accident that all the largest-circulation newspapers in West Africa, and the most prestigious newspapers in India, are printed in English.

I say this, not in a spirit of pride, or because things are necessarily going to remain so, but because it is necessary to see overseas writing in English today in this sort of perspective. Whereas none would now challenge the validity of North American or Australian creative expression in English, the charge is too often brought against African or Indian writers in this medium (especially by people of no literary perception) that they are somehow engaged in an irrelevant and totally unrepresentative activity. In so far as their lives are touched by the language, and made aware through it of an audience transcending tribe, state or region, I believe that they are in fact sincerely representative of a large and ever-growing proportion of their own generation. And this must be said without in any way diminishing the complementary importance of writing in Urdu, Hindi, Bengali, Swahili, Yoruba or a hundred other languages.

The case, then, for adding an overseas dimension to English studies in the United Kingdom is such as I have outlined above. The recognition of American literature (by which, incidentally, is too often meant the literature of the U.S.A. alone) is only the first step along this path, and in recent years several universities have recognized that it is an inadequate step. The time may not have come for setting up grandly-named institutes for the study of Ghanaian or Jamaican or Kenyan literature, but it has certainly come for taking cognizance of the more important literary achievements in English stemming from Africa, Southern Asia and the Caribbean as a whole. It may be worth noting that Spain and Portugal already face a situation where most of the important writers of their languages are to be found in the Americas. Complacent notions of the 'metropolitan' and the 'provincial' are meaningless when applied to writers like Pablo Neruda of Chile, Octavio Paz of Mexico or Jorge Luis Borges of Argentina. Likewise, many would consider contemporary North American poetry and fiction to have a decided edge over what England itself can now produce.

**University studies**

University studies in England of any overseas English writing, other than North American, are barely ten years old. In 1959 the School of English at Leeds initiated a programme of studies in Commonwealth literature which was certainly the pioneer venture in this field. Leeds has also been able to act as host to a number of visiting writers and scholars from India, Africa and the Caribbean and to hold an important conference on Commonwealth Writing in 1964. More recently, a number of other universities have found means of incorporating some study of overseas English writing with their undergraduate courses; these include Edinburgh, Sussex and Kent. Several more universities have recognized the subject to the extent of accepting graduate studies in this field.

The precise method and degree of incorporation is bound to vary according to whether the university concerned has its courses divided up into single-subject honours schools, into groupings of similar subjects or into regional studies. There are difficulties and advantages about all these arrangements. The 'Commonwealth' concept employed at Leeds, for example, has the advantage of neatness. It may, however, seem to link unlike things together and to make an apparent separation between areas of genuine likeness. How valid is it, for example, to divide the literature of North America into 'American' (i.e. U.S.A.) and 'Commonwealth' (i.e. Canadian) compartments, which may come to be studied in separate programmes? Another difficulty, of course, is that much of the best Canadian literature is appearing in French anyway, and in what sense could this literature be brought within the scope of any course on overseas writing in English? Again, militant black American writers like Eldridge Cleaver and Le Roi Jones, who are specifically concerned to internationalize the discussion of race, to take it out of the purely national context in which it has for too long been looked at within the United States, might be felt to have more in common with other militant black writers elsewhere, moved by similar concerns, than with their white American contemporaries. Likewise, the emerging literature of Australia, being that of another wealthy, predominantly white and predominantly middle-class culture, is likely to have more in common with that of white America than with anything coming from its immediate 'Commonwealth' neighbours such as Papua and New Guinea, Singapore and Malaysia.

Another possibility is to group together all overseas writing in English under some such title as 'Anglophone'. This has the advantage of drawing no line between non-Commonwealth areas like the Philippines, where much writing in English is also appearing, and their Commonwealth neighbours. It also gets rid of the slightly loaded word 'English', which is apt to carry with it suspicions of latter-day cultural colonization by the old imperial power. But its great shortcoming is that it tends to separate the activity of writing in English from every-thing else that is going on in these societies; from everything, in fact, that the writers are writing *about*. For, anywhere in Africa or Asia, the sectors of national life and activity to which the word Anglophone can be applied are inevitably limited ones.

This is where regionally-based studies display their strong point. It is easy to minimize the extent to which we effortlessly assume a great deal of knowledge about our own history, culture, values and environment whenever we look critically at a piece of English literature. When we read an Indian novel, a Guyanese poem or a Nigerian play, this kind of knowledge is not available to us, and it would be false to argue that we ought not to need it if the work is good enough. Clearly there are great advantages in linking the study of literature in a par-ticular region with parallel studies in its history, social institu-tions, culture and intellectual traditions. This is something that the regional organization of courses makes possible, an organization which has been adopted in various forms by several of the newer British universities. A penalty for this very comprehensiveness is that it cuts into the time available for purely literary study within the rather narrow limits of an undergraduate course. It will therefore appeal more to those who seek the kind of integrated approach to the literary study of a region (e.g. Africa, Southern Asia or the Caribbean) than to those who wish to concentrate upon the tools of a particular critical discipline.

## Language and experience

It would be possible to argue that some acquaintance with the achievements of this overseas literature in English is necessary to anyone who interests himself in the range of expression of which the language is capable. Just as the dialect poems of Robert Burns or William Barnes will illuminate some of the problems and practices of the modern West Indian poet, so a study of contemporary dialect poetry helps us to place Burns and Barnes in a tradition which is not simply regional, but is part of the continuing development of a language always remarkable for its flexibility, its lack of inflection and its openness to new words and idioms. This tradition runs right through the eighteenth and nineteenth centuries, in the bush-whackers' ballads of Australia; the spirituals, work-songs, shanties and cowboy ballads of America; the rich folk-song of the Caribbean area; and on into the twentieth century, in forms like calypso, blues and mento.

We have seen how Derek Walcott derives part of his irony from his very awareness of English literature and his sense of its displacement in the tropical Caribbean:

in a green world, one without metaphors;

Another West Indian poet of today, Edward Brathwaite, is concerned to bring his poetry into direct relationship with those traditions of folk speech and song outlined above. The richest canon of English folk poetry since the sixteenth century is undoubtedly that produced by the black man in the Americas.

Brathwaite feels this entire achievement, ranging over three centuries and the whole sweep of the continent, to be part of his heritage as a black man raised in the little island of Barbados. In his major poetic trilogy, *Rights of Passage*, *Masks* and *Islands* (published between 1967 and 1969), he selects from that heritage at various points, dependent on the mood and tempo he is seeking to evoke. Here is a passage from *Islands* in which he uses as a refrain the well-known song 'I want somebody limbo like me' as a ground-base for his poem about the impulse towards racial rebirth after the dark night of slavery and exile. Limbo itself, though now degraded to a nightclub entertainment, is a former *rite de passage*, or initiation dance, which was part of the death ceremonies in many parts of the Caribbean. The celebrant has to dance, inch by inch, under a low stick held parallel with the ground. He must pass right under the stick and spring upright again without touching it; clearly an analogue for rebirth and the transcendence of death. Hence the original meaning of the dance, which under- lies its popular modern lyric, helps to inform and shape the meaning of the poem:[2]

> And limbo stick is the silence in front of me
> *limbo*
>
> long dark deck and the water surrounding me
> long dark deck and the silence is over me
>
> *limbo*
> *limbo like me*
>
> stick is the whip
> and the dark deck is slavery
>
> stick is the whip
> and the dark deck is slavery
>
> *limbo*
> *limbo like me*
>
> drum stick knock
> and the darkness is over me
>
> knees spread wide
> and the water is hiding me
>
> *limbo*
> *limbo like me*
>
> knees spread wide
> and dark ground is under me
>
> down
> down
> down
>
> and the drummer is calling me

*limbo*
*limbo like me*

sun coming up
and the drummers are praising me

out of the dark
and the dumb gods are raising me

up
up
up

and the music is saving me

hot
slow
step

on the burning ground

This is a good example of how Brathwaite invokes the whole context of black experience in the New World, and the patterns of verbal expression that record it, as the material of his poetry. He has been able to extend vastly the resources available to a poet in the language, in a way that might seem mere exoticism in a white writer, in one who had not participated in the experience which created these resources.

The study of overseas literature in English also enables us to see how the language responds, not only to the challenge of an alien temperament and experience (for here we already have Conrad and the Irish writers to inform us), but to the definition of lives in which English, even in dialect form, is unknown. When an African or Indian novelist writes of village life, he is not carrying out a refinement and selection of everyday speech such as every artist must attempt, but is constantly seeking verbal *equivalents* for languages whose tonal and grammatical structure, whose rhythmic shape, whose whole approach to the ordering of experience, are fundamentally different from those of English. This might not matter so much for the novelist seeking to express his own alienation, to register his otherness from what he describes. But this essentially colonial type of writing, in which the author reports to us, his European audience, upon the curious antics of his former countrymen, is now happily dead; unless it lingers on in the work of V. S. Naipaul. If the mere act of writing in English is not to be, for an African or Indian, a colonial performance in itself, then he must show his readers that his cloak of language is invisible, that it does not prevent him from moving into the heart of his subject and speaking from there, even if his English words might be unintelligible to those immediately around him.

In Africa, where the approach to writing in English has generally been less formal and literary than in India, a number of different devices have been adopted for communicating with the reader of English and yet reminding him that the experience he is encountering has a quality and tempo of its own. One of the more extreme experiments is that of the Nigerian poet Gabriel Okara in his novel *The Voice*. Okara was clearly trying to convey in English something about the sequence in which experience is perceived by his people (the Ijaw) and transmitted through language, a sequence which naturally differs somewhat from that embodied in standard English usage. Certain Ijaw concepts which do not have precise English equivalents are also translated directly, so that the effect is to challenge the reader to recognize the unfamiliar and grapple with its meaning. Words such as 'head', 'inside', 'breath', 'word' and 'shadow' are placed in contexts which create a sense of strangeness and show the reader that he is dealing with a symbolic language in which a new or fuller significance must be attached to them. For traditional Africa views the world, not as so much inert matter interspersed with autonomous and separate living organisms, but as a vast system of spiritually-charged objects and beings where everything interacts through correspondence and analogy. Hence no act is autonomous, and any act is capable of disturbing the general harmony if carried out in disregard of it. The following passage[3] conveys something of this effect:

You asked me why I am giving you my hands in the happening-thing, when you have become the enemy of everything in the town? Well, I am giving you my hands and my inside and even my shadow to let them see in their insides that if even the people do not know, we, you and I, know and have prepared our bodies to stand in front of them and tell them so . . . Then you returned, and when I started to hear the happening-things in your name, my hopes rose to the eye of the sky. And then yesterday you came running, being pursued by the people. So I called you in. These are my answering words to your questioning words.

A fellow Ijaw writer, John Pepper Clark, has criticized effects like these as 'sounding more like German than either Ijaw or English'. He points out that Okara is not consistent in his re-arrangements of syntax and that some of his most beautiful passages rely for their effect upon imagery rather than upon inversions of word-order or strange coinages like 'happening-things'. There is some justice in these charges, though Okara has succeeded in reminding his non-Ijaw readers that there are some genuinely different concepts to be encountered in Africa, not in a mere spirit of exoticism, but in the search for real understanding of what shapes character, motive and action in these societies.

Clark himself has attempted the transliteration of a traditional Ijaw text in his version of the Ozidi saga, an epic recited over seven consecutive nights, with music, dance and mime, in certain villages of the Niger Delta. Although he attempts nothing as extreme as some of Okara's devices, he has still felt the need to render something of the different sequence in which speech or action may present themselves in an African vernacular. The result is probably closer to a literal translation of what the Ijaw words actually mean than it is to the poetic re-arrangements of Okara:[4]

> Now in the district of Ozidi there were no people. All the people were dead. He and his brother alone were left. With them like that, the townspeople after looking steadily at the matter, spoke out:
> 'Yes, with the matter as it is, if we fail to name our next king from that ward, we would have insulted them. Because of that, let us go there and install in Ozidi's district a king.'
> Now the brother of Ozidi, Temugedege was his name . . .

Again, the effect is to remind us that we are encountering differences, rather than to lull us into a false sense of familiarity. But the Clark approach carries its own dangers, for the translation, however faithful, may nevertheless come out sounding like a bit of sub-Tolkien. The writer who has generally been thought most successful in rendering certain qualities of African speech without falling into bizarre or distracting effects is the Nigerian novelist Chinua Achebe. For his narrative passages he depends upon a simple, direct style of 'standard' English, distinguished from the familiar only by its subject matter and by the occasional use of a word which resists translation into English: *obi, egwugwu, ikenga, okpara.* But Achebe's dialogue, particularly in his scenes of village life, always has a weight and a deliberate tempo of its own. Like most African vernacular speech, of the older generation, it is highly allusive, continually validating its judgments by brief references to what is commonly known in that community, continually underlining its advice with proverbial authority. Here is a typical passage from Achebe's third novel, *Arrow of God,*[5] where the speaker warns his hearers not to resist conscription for labour on a new road:

> do you forget that this is the moon of planting? Do you want to grow this year's crops in the prison house in a land where your fathers owe a cow? I speak as your elder brother. I have travelled in Olu and I have travelled in Igbo, and I can tell you that there is no escape from the white man. He has come. When Suffering knocks at your door and you say there is no seat left for him, he tells you not to worry because he has brought his own stool. The white man is like that. Before any of you were old enough to tie a cloth between the legs I saw with my own eyes what the white man did to Abame. Then I knew that there was no escape. As daylight chases away darkness so will the white man drive away all our customs. I know that as I say it now it passes by your ears, but it will happen.

The quality of the writing is impressive; with its density of concrete illustration, its dignity and deep sincerity, it is typical of Achebe's mature style. It can convey passionate anger as well as wisdom, sardonic humour as well as religious contemplation, but it has been criticized as failing to render the joy and animal high spirits which are also part of African life. There is something a little grim about it, like a finely-cut Ibo mask, full of form, beauty and power, yet concealing the rounded flesh beneath. The problem, not entirely resolved despite all Achebe's skill, is to achieve weight without creating an effect of heaviness.

The Guinea Coast of West Africa, from which several of our examples have been taken, has enjoyed a long and complex relationship with the English language; a relationship which goes far beyond a formal literary instruction in the school-room. The lively and diverse dialects of 'pidgin English', which are found all along the coast from Freetown to the Cameroons, are the product of generations of English usage acquired through trade and other contacts, rather than through education. Alongside these, there exists the ebulliently inventive but unorthodox English of the popular bookstall literature, often described as 'Onitsha novelettes', full of phrases like 'he daggered himself to death' or 'he hurled her into his knees'. The predominant influences here are from the cinema, newspapers and illustrated magazines. Beyond this again is the colloquial and fluent English often spoken by highly-educated West Africans among themselves, such as Wole Soyinka employs in his novel *The Interpreters*. Finally, there is the stiff and circumlocutory formal English of civil service and other officialdom. Everyday English usage in West Africa thus ranges from the lorry-park and the market place to the university common room and the debating chamber. West African writers have been able to take advantage of this variety by representing every one of these levels and types of English in their work, together with any original arrangements of the language which they may make in their efforts to render vernacular speech.

If we turn now to India, we shall find a rather different linguistic situation surrounding the writer of English. There are estimated to be some nine million speakers of English in India, many of them Eurasians who hold it as their native language. But then there are also some hundreds of millions of Indians who neither speak nor read English at all, even though they may have enjoyed several years of education and be literate in their own languages. Again, because the major Indian languages had been written for many centuries before there was any contact with Europe, there is no correlation in the public mind between the tools of literacy and the impact of a foreign language and educational system. Although large parts of Africa had been penetrated by Arabic scholars from the late middle ages onwards, this was an arcane skill confined to a small class of literati and never amounted to the announcement of an entirely new social order, as did the introduction of English missionary and government schools during the past hundred years. English is also the language of instruction in secondary schools and universities over most of former British Africa. Thus, although there is now a good deal of literary activity in the major African languages, as in those of India, it would be true to say that most of the best-known authors write in English, thereby gaining for themselves at once a national, a pan-African and an international audience.

The situation is otherwise in India, where many of those who write in English have either settled in Europe, like Ved Mehta, Kamala Markandya and Raja Rao, or have spent considerable periods of their lives there, like Balachandra Rajan, and Santha Rama Rao. Within India, their work exists alongside that of many established and best-selling novelists and poets writing exclusively in languages such as Hindi, Gujarati, Mahrathi and Bengali. Although there has been some excellent creative work done in English, this overall situation is bound to affect both the attitude of the writer himself towards his audience and material, and the attitude of the reading public towards his activity. Added to this is the difficulty of finding an acceptable English style in a situation where English expression is often either stiff, literary and rather archaic or else broken, fragmentary and incorrect.

To see the strength of this literary tradition surrounding (or perhaps embedding) English in India, it is sufficient to look at the opening pages of a book like Nirad Chaudhuri's *A Passage to England*. Even this highly sophisticated Indian cannot land on the shores of England without an obscuring veil of Milton, Wordsworth and Keats falling between him and the contemporary reality that confronts him.

One Indian poet writing in English, Dr Mokashi Punekar,

has made a bold effort to break out of this literary stranglehold by developing a style which shocks the expectations of both his Indian and his English readers. Whereas an Oxonian Indian poet like Dom Moraes beguiles us by the very smoothness and colloquial assurance of his English practice, this writer seems determined to work out his own rules and pay no homage to the 'metropolitan' muse:

> The keen heart gets hard like the stone in almond skin
> Leaving sweet gaps between for work to home.
> Food creates its feeder, itch its poetic gnome:
> Why not virtues incipience in so sweet a sin?

The effect is halting and rebarbative, yet the suspicion that this is mere inadvertent clumsiness doesn't survive a fuller examination of his poetry. His choice of words and rhythms is deliberate; it forces us back upon the question of how far English prosody is bound up with the rhythms and patterns of verbal association developed in these islands. Poets like Eliot or Walcott come into the tradition and use these rhythms and patterns for purposes of their own, but in ways that deliberately invoke the tradition itself. Brathwaite, on the other hand, has appealed to another tradition in English altogether, that of black folk poetry, speech and song in the New World. He claims the same freedom that their nameless innovators have already claimed. Yet all three of these poets grew up in English-speaking communities and relate at some point to a living system of English usage. Mokashi Punekar comes from no such system and rejects the embrace of purely literary usage which many of his fellow writers have accepted as a substitute for it. It is interesting to compare his work with that of another Indian poet, who did grow up in an English-speaking community within India, Laurence Bantleman:[6]

> Are we too lucky Stuart since
> We've missed our bus – sadly? Oh no
> Not sadly, actually it is
> The bitch that sinners call experience.
> We can still dance, yes we still can
> (Fully aware that no-one's gentle cum a man).

Here there is obviously more common ground between Indian

I

poet and English reader; the effect is vaguely metaphysical, but there are certain things about the lines (the ambiguity of 'too', the placing of that first 'sadly' and the startling, rather bookish use of 'cum') that seem to jog the reader into an awareness that he is encountering a foreign tradition of English usage, and not a mere outpost of 'Eng. Lit.' implanted by the British Council.

There remains the consideration of the so-called white dominions, where supposedly everyone, except the French Canadians, is a native speaker of English. In fact, however, we already have some Maori and Australian Aborigine poets who write English as a foreign language, and these may soon be joined by a Canadian Eskimo or two. Nevertheless, we are dealing here with literatures where there is virtually no choice but to write in English and where development of a distinctive national tradition may be expected to follow a pattern rather similar to that of the United States. It took over two hundred years for America to produce writers as native as Mark Twain and Walt Whitman, but the process looks like being a little quicker in Australia, Canada and New Zealand. The days are over when a 'colonial' writer had to assimilate more or less to the English literary scene, as Katherine Mansfield of New Zealand did in the 1920s, in order to get any recognition. The novelist Patrick White, though he too went through his 'English' period, emerges as aggressively Australian in a book like *Voss*. Australian poetry, too, assisted for many years by the pioneer magazine *Meanjin*, has acquired a definite independence and authority, qualities which are now becoming apparent in the poetry of New Zealand also.

For a Canadian writer like Mordecai Richler, the problem may be to differentiate himself (if he wants to) from what is happening south of the 49th Parallel. Cultural debate in English-speaking Canada is currently torn between the acceptance of an overall 'North American' identity and the fierce avowal of a Canadian separateness, with or without its French-speaking component. The natural public of a successful Canadian writer is a North American one, of which his Canadian readers form less than a tenth. But for this very reason the development of Canadian writing over the next few years will make a study of particular interest.

## Critical approaches

Enough has been said to indicate something of the variety of form, preoccupation and experience to be encountered in overseas writing in English. Until very recent years, many of these writers have operated locally in something of a critical vacuum. They have suffered from the usual colonial tendency to await the accolade of metropolitan approval before giving honour to a fellow-citizen. In England itself, reviewers often ignored their work if it was genuinely challenging and new, or praised it exaggeratedly for reasons which had little to do with literature. Praise of this kind tends to turn a book into a nine-days' wonder, followed by an interval of oblivion from which it only emerges as a remaindered edition in the cut-price bookshops. For the sake of real critical appraisal, it is often better for an author to make his way more slowly into esteem, but for this he will need the assistance of critics who are prepared to work at him, to read and reread his books several times and patiently expose their structure and their meaning.

With the development of university studies in this literature, both here and in many other parts of the English-speaking world, the prospects for this kind of recognition and selection have been improved and the new literature of, for instance, Africa and the West Indies is in less danger of being treated as some kind of exotic freak which demands nothing but shrieks of amazement.

Most valuable of all has been the emergence of that indigenous criticism which is the only soil in which a writer can grow, without the distortion that comes from turning his blooms towards an alien sunlight. Domestic criticism had first to free itself from that inferiority complex which often caused it to diminish and undervalue the local product. The rise of nationalist emotion carries the contrary dangers of inflation, as well as clamorous demands for the wrong kind of 'commitment' from those who understand politics better than literature. Here the true critic can help by never ceasing to stress that the writer's greatest commitment, far transcending this or that external and ephemeral cause, is to his own integrity, his own vision of truth. But these processes can only begin when both writer and critic are ready to fasten their gaze primarily upon their own society; when Sydney, Bombay, Lagos or Port-of-Spain begin to seem metropolis enough for their encounter.

The development of a vigorous school of criticism in the writer's own country is bound to bring in its train questions about the stance an English critic (or an English university student) should adopt when confronted with, say, an Indian novel or a Nigerian poetic drama. It is possible to answer with a Johnsonian forthrightness that he should just blast right ahead and criticize the fellow exactly as he would anyone else who ventures to write in English. At the other extreme, he may fall over backwards in his efforts to adopt vicariously the posture of an Indian or an African reader. In India, for example, the demand that literature should be didactic, reticent and finally on the side of traditional virtues is quite as strong as it was in Victorian England. Cyril Connolly long ago advised English readers to seek no other quality in a modern writer than 'the resonance of his despair'. Such advice will hardly commend itself in countries where collective idealism has not yet surrendered to the demands of the individual psyche for endless self-examination, or to the romantic cult of the outsider who rejoices in his own alienation. Nor does it follow, in literature or in any other sphere, that developments in these countries are bound to follow in time the patterns set in Western Europe or North America: part of the stimulation and the challenge of these new literatures is that they probably won't.

The answer to our question, if one can be attempted at present, is that ultimately the critic must judge the work before him by the light of his own experience and his own sympathy; but that experience and that sympathy may themselves be greatly enlarged by the encounter. A carefully acquired knowledge of what, culturally and historically, lies around and behind a given work from overseas is certainly not a non-literary irrelevance. It will not be easy to acquire, but in so far as we can acquire it, we shall probably increase our purely literary enjoyment and understanding of what we read. Knowledge of this kind will not help to turn the reader into an Indian, an Australian or a Jamaican; but it should turn him into a better student, and a better critic.

## Notes

1. 'Crusoe's Journal', *The Castaway*, Cape, 1965, 51.
2. 'Limbo', *Islands*, O.U.P., 1969, 37–8.
3. *The Voice*, André Deutsch, 1964, 55–6.
4. 'The Ozidi Saga', in *Black Orpheus*, vol. 2, no. 2, June–September 1968.
5. *Arrow of God*, Heinemann, 1964, 104–5.
6. I am indebted to Mr David McCutchion for the quotations from Dr Mokashi's *The Captive* and Laurence Bantleman's *Graffiti*, both published in India.

# 7

# The Place of American Literature

*Andrew Hook*

The *Journal of English and Germanic Philology* is still very much
with us though its contents now (fortunately) belie its title.
None the less no academic periodical exists with a title better
suited to suggest all that has been dry, desiccated, and dreary
in English studies. The story of how English as a subject threw
off its early concern for rhetoric and 'style' – how to write
elegantly and correctly – and assumed its place as a scholarly
'discipline' by a strong infusion of Germanic philology on the
one hand and Teutonic methodology on the other is well
enough known. But nowhere is the retreat of English Studies
into a hidebound conservatism of attitude and approach, itself
a consequence of its exponents' uneasiness over their subject's
status as a valid academic discipline, more clearly and dis-
tressingly illustrated than in the case of American literature.

In 1866 a Liverpool gentleman named Henry Yates Thompson offered to endow a lectureship at Cambridge in the
'History, Literature, and Institutions of the United States', the
lecturer to be appointed by the President and Fellows of
Harvard. Whether or not it was this last point that caused the
trouble, the fact remains that for a combination of academic,
political and ecclesiastical reasons the offer was rejected as a
dangerous novelty. Not far short of another hundred years was
to pass before American literature, that dangerous novelty,
was to be timorously admitted into the company of legitimate
English studies. Certainly it was no earlier than the 1950s that
the study of American literature began to appear in the

curricula of certain venturous English universities. Only in the 1960s could one *expect* to discover American literature appearing somewhere in the curriculum of a British university. And even now the chances are that it will appear as an Honours option, or a special topic, or an optional paper, or something of the kind.

Is there any justification for the pusillanimity and tardiness of this British welcome to the literature of the United States? Not in my opinion. In American history it is possible to distinguish between times in which the Constitution is broadly or narrowly interpreted: in times of broad interpretation the Supreme Court extends its power to regulate whatever areas of American life are not explicitly denied it by the Constitution; in times of narrow interpretation, on the contrary, the Court limits itself to the consideration of those areas specifically assigned to it by the Constitution. In English literature a similar broad or narrow definition of its proper jurisdiction seems to operate. From a broad historical perspective the narrow definition has apparently prevailed: English literature is neither more nor less than the literature of England. But narrowness may have in fact concealed breadth. In accordance with such a definition of the limits of English literature England seems to be capable of a quite remarkable geographical extension. Take the example of English drama. At the end of the Elizabethan and Jacobean high season who are the most eminent inheritors and sustainers of the English dramatic tradition? Surely such playwrights as Congreve, Farquhar, Sheridan, Wilde, Shaw, O'Casey, and Beckett – Irishmen to a man. To put it another way, English literature has never experienced the slightest difficulty in embracing and assimilating all that is best in Scottish, Irish, and Welsh literature. In few areas is the blandness of imperial self-confidence better illustrated.

If English literature has been ready and willing enough to encompass the literatures of Great Britain and Ireland why should the literature of America have been for so long regarded as a dangerous and unwelcome novelty? To answer that question adequately would involve a lengthy digression into the course of Anglo-American social and political relations throughout most of the nineteenth century. In particular it would involve detailed consideration of the so-called 'literary quarrel' between England and America extending on beyond the middle of the century and conducted in the main in the pages of a variety of literary periodicals on both sides of the Atlantic. The literary quarrel raged – and it really did – over such topics as the status of American literary culture, books describing the American scene written by British travellers in America, and of course America's political significance. If to the intense and enduring ill-feeling represented by the literary quarrel is added the disgruntlement of numerous British authors over American republication of their books which, in the absence of any international copyright law, earned them nothing, we can appreciate why for most of the nineteenth century American literature, despite English admiration for a few American authors, should have been looked upon with very mixed feelings indeed. For example, had Scott received a penny for every volume sold in America his bankruptcy would never have occurred and he would have written fewer Waverley novels.

But what is understandable in the nineteenth century is much less so in the twentieth. The neglect of American literature in our schools, colleges, and universities, until the very recent past, represents nothing more than traditional academic conservatism and narrow-mindedness. After all, the achievement of American literature in the middle of the twentieth century is a very different matter from what it was at the opening of the nineteenth. In 1820, with the literary quarrel already in full swing, Sydney Smith of the *Edinburgh Review*, the critical sledge-hammer of its day, infuriated America by asking one question: 'Who reads an American book?' The shot at Lexington marking the opening of the American Revolution is supposed to be the shot that echoed round the world. One may doubt whether in America itself it echoed any louder than Sydney Smith's dismissive question. As the *Edinburgh Review* put it a little later:

We really thought at one time they would have fitted out an armament against the *Edinburgh* and *Quarterly Reviews*, and burnt down Mr Murray's and Mr Constable's shops, as we did the American Capitol. We, however, remember no other

anti-American crime of which we were guilty, than a pre-
ference of Shakespeare and Milton over Joel Barlow and
Timothy Dwight.

For Americans the exasperating point, no doubt, was that
Sydney Smith and the *Edinburgh Review* were perfectly correct.
No one did read an American book. In 1820 American literature was little more than a promise, a hope for the future. The
Joel Barlows and Timothy Dwights certainly existed, but the
existence of writers is not quite synonymous with the existence
of a viable literature.

How different is the situation today. We all read American
books. The prophecy of Constable's *Edinburgh Magazine*, also
made in 1820, has been more than fulfilled:

> We should not be much surprised were we to live to see the
> day when we, in our turn shall be gaping for new novels and
> poems from the other side of the Atlantic, and when, in the
> silence of our own bards and romancers, we shall have Ladies
> of the Lake from Ontario, and Tales of My Landlord from
> Goose-creek, as a counterpart to those from Gandercleugh.

While Scott has not in fact succeeded in silencing all subsequent
British writers 'new novels and poems from the other side of the
Atlantic' have long been part of our normal reading. In fact it
is difficult to over-estimate the significance of American writing
in the twentieth century. The most important aspect of the
literature of this century is the rise of the 'modern movement'
(now over) focused as far as literature in English goes in the
work of such writers as Eliot, Yeats, Pound, Joyce, and Lawrence. But a good case can be made for the view that the
modern movement was largely American in origin and inspiration. What this means is that the contemporary student who
takes an intelligent interest in recent writing (and can a serious
student *not* be interested in recent and contemporary writing?)
will inevitably find himself reading American books.

In modern poetry, for example, the contributions of Eliot
and Pound were decisive. Between them they went a long way
towards producing a new poetry and a new criticism to go with
it. But the main point is not the academic one of the precise
nature and extent of the American contribution to the modern

movement in twentieth-century literary history. Rather it is the reiteration of the basic fact that in this century it has been impossible not to read American books. Consider the case of the novel. It may well be true that in the twentieth century America has produced only one novelist who might rank with the great European exponents of the form such as Joyce, Proust, Mann, or Lawrence: I mean William Faulkner. But one suspects that Faulkner has in fact been less widely read and less influential in this country than a considerable number of American novelists not quite of his eminence. Hemingway and Fitzgerald, for example, of his own generation, Salinger and Saul Bellow of a younger one. Once again the question is not one of a few distinguished names. The American novel in this century is characterized by such fantastic richness, variety, and vitality, and is the work of such a range of schools and methods – Southern, Jewish, Negro, realist, naturalist, symbolist – that it has become a kind of vast Moby Dick disporting itself in the seas of 'Eng. Lit.' perhaps at the expense of the lesser fish of other countries.

The present reality is undoubtedly that to consider studying or teaching modern English literature without taking into account the American contribution is to indulge a rather provincial insularity. American literature has existed for about 300 years; and has been particularly lively for the last 150 or so. That university departments concerned with literary studies in English for so long successfully refused to acknowledge that existence is now interesting but irrelevant. The dust of old battles may be left undisturbed. The revolution is now, and most British universities allow the study of American literature some place in the sun. Henry Yates Thompson at least would be pleased.

American literature may have been finally admitted to our universities, but how familiar is the average sixth-former or even undergraduate with its characteristics, its variety, its forms? Apart from slick sex-and-violence paperbacks does American literature suggest much more than the odd modern novel, 'Hiawatha', and half-forgotten boys' adventure stories: *The Last of the Mohicans, Tom Sawyer* and *Huckleberry Finn, The Red Badge of Courage,* and drastically abridged versions of *Moby Dick*? In most cases probably not much. Why then should the student be encouraged not only to read but to *study* American literature? With what kind of expectations should he approach that reading and study? What are the qualities of American literature that make it not only historically significant but intellectually and imaginatively rewarding? Why is the experience of American writing ultimately valuable? Such questions are fundamental to any consideration of the place of American literature in English Studies. The student who is perhaps facing a choice between American literature and one of the areas or periods of English literature wants to know what the choice of American literature will mean; what he has let himself in for and what he can reasonably expect to find.

In the first place such a student will find of course that a 'poem is a poem is a poem'. English and American literature have an immense amount in common: a shared language, a shared literary heritage, and to some extent a shared cultural tradition. Hence an American poem or an American novel is available to the English reader in the way that a foreign litera-ture is not. The English student requires no special knowledge, no special preparation; all that is required of him is that he pick up the American text and begin. But here the trouble may start. If on the basis of the fundamental similarities I have mentioned he assumes that his experience of the American text will be identical with that of an English one he is liable to be disappointed. Alongside the major likenesses are differences of a rather subtle and sophisticated nature which the literary student in particular needs to be alert to. American literature is not in general English literature which happens to have been written three thousand miles away across the Atlantic. American contributions to the modern movement, and the consequent interrelatedness of many aspects of English and American literary culture in the twentieth century, should not blind us to the differences between the two literatures. No reader or critic would approach a novel in English written in Jamaica or West Africa or New Delhi with expectations wholly uninfluenced by its place of origin. Similarly then with regard to a novel written in New York or Boston, not to mention Chicago or Los Angeles.

I should regard it as axiomatic that a writer's imaginative

vision is in some way related to the nature of his experience. In this sense life and art do inter-penetrate. The experience of the American writer is itself the product of his environment in its broadest sense, the configuration of his political, social, economic, intellectual and many other realities. It is these realities that go towards the defining of the wider vessel inside which the individual consciousness is formed. That vessel is not, in the case of the English and American writer, co-extensive. In other words the American writer's experience is wholly other than that of his English counterpart. From the moment that the original settlers sailed for the New World the English and American experiences have diverged. The American Revolution and the formal severing of the political and social ties between the countries is only the most dramatic affirmation of the difference.

Only because the difference is there does it become possible to talk of the existence of American literature. Whether there was in fact an American literature was once a favourite joke question. In Oscar Wilde's *A Woman of No Importance* a character is described as having made his money in American dry goods. Asked for a definition of 'dry goods' the fast answer is: 'American novels.' And certainly as the American academic mill grinds finer and finer one does sometimes begin to wonder whether American literature really is a question of a Middle-Western professor compiling yet another exhaustive (and exhausting) bibliography of the forgotten writings of yet another forgotten minor American 'realist' or 'naturalist' or 'humorist' or 'local colorist' or 'regionalist'. Dry goods indeed. But the existence of an American literature rests on a more substantial basis than that of the compilation and 'critical' analyses of the works of literary nonentities who by geographical chance have put pen to paper on the banks of the Hudson, or the Ohio, or the Mississippi. American literature exists because over the last two centuries or so the literary imagination has striven to reflect, comprehend, envision and embody the American experience. In the nineteenth century in particular the literary imagination seems to have been vivified by the idea of America: in the works of Cooper, Hawthorne, Melville, Emerson, Whitman, Twain, and Henry James the imagination's creative power shines forth momentarily, fitfully, or with sustained effect. Geographical chance made these men, too, American; but the literature they wrote is American literature because the forms which define and create their imaginative visions are both reflexions of their American experience and attempts to comprehend America imaginatively. Their works are American in subject-matter, American in form, and American in expression.

Precisely in terms of subject-matter, however, what does it mean to suggest that American literature tries to comprehend America? Does it mean simply that American literature is about America? In a sense, yes. Just how surprising such a notion is emerges if we try to imagine a literary critic or historian suggesting that English literature is English because its subject is England. Why then risk the apparent absurdity of suggesting that American literature is about America? Ultimately because, compared with the majority of European countries, America is as a nation and society amazingly self-conscious. It did not evolve or develop; in 1776 by divine *fiat*, as it were, the United States of America was instantly created. The New World was once again made new. To be American was to be conscious of just this. What is true of the nation is true of its literature. Of course, a colonial American literature had existed long before 1776, but its connexion with what comes after is not specially striking. Equally, long after 1776 a great deal of literature was produced in America that was no more than a limp imitation of the standard English models of a decade or two earlier. But the American literature we read today reflects neither a colonial heritage nor any submission to English literary values. It is new and different. And a striking aspect of its difference is its surprising alertness to the significance of 1776: to the attempt to create and define a new country, to establish, even to write down, what its nature and potential should be; to announce a society with a prescribed commitment to essential human values. It is as though the boldness of such an American experiment was itself a challenge to the literary imagination. Certainly most American writing of creative value in the nineteenth century – and much in the twentieth century too – is marked by a subtle exploration and testing of the questions and issues raised by 1776. The individual and society; the world of hope, aspiration, vision or dream and the world of reality and

necessity; man and nature; such great over-riding themes of
the literary imagination at all times and in all places were given
a special freshness and relevance for the American writer by
the fact of the existence of America. If 1776 was the dream,
what was the reality? What are life, liberty, and the pursuit of
happiness? A cheat and a delusion, or a powerful satiric norm?
An expression of man's deepest aspirations and longings? Or
a complacently optimistic *naïveté*, blind to the radical imper-
fections of human nature? Is the freedom of the individual
finally compatible with any conceivable social structure? The
questions are sharp and meaningful because they emerge from
the very context of American life. They are what the American
experiment is about. Hardly surprising then that the American
creative imagination should have been preoccupied with them.
They constitute, as it were, the 'matter of America', the
given materials out of which the artist creates his individual
vision.

The major writers of nineteenth-century America – and a
great many minor ones – were centrally concerned with the
nature of America and the American and all that these implied,
and subsequent generations of American writers have never
abandoned the topic. Even today it is possible to feel that the
note of bitterness and contempt and even hatred for America
and American society, so characteristic of current American
writing, both white and black, owes much to the sense that
America is a broken promise, a self-betrayal; that in its injustices, inequalities, its violence and cruelty, America denies
the principles which provided its original definition.

If one may digress a moment I should say at this point that
it is its continuing preoccupation with the idea of America that
justifies the inclusion of American literature within the framework of what is generally called American Studies. American
Studies draws on a variety of academic disciplines to try to
illuminate the nature of American culture and society in all its
aspects. American history, geography, economics, politics,
sociology, all have much to contribute; but it is perhaps in
American literature that the truest, most searching analysis of
America is to be found. Hence it is appropriate that the study
of American writing should be the corner-stone of the kind of
comprehensive, inter-disciplinary area study of America that

provides a valuable addition to the traditional specialisms of the English Honours type.

The point I have been trying to make about how the idea of America provided and goes on providing American literature with a particularly sharp focus for certain fundamental human concerns and questions may be used to illustrate another recurring feature of American writing. Questions about man and his relationship to nature or to God; about individual freedom and social constraint; about human perfectibility or fallibility; about the nature of reality itself – such questions are hardly the exclusive prerogative of the literary artist. Philosophers and metaphysicians might well be more at home with them. Yet themes related to such questions are commonplace in American literature, and in American fiction in particular. The English novelist, on the other hand, is not usually thought of in relation to the philosopher or metaphysician; if he rubs shoulders with workers in other fields it would be with the sociologist, the social scientist or historian. The English novel provides an unparalleled evocation of and commentary upon English society. The pages of Jane Austen, Dickens, Thackeray, Trollope, and George Eliot provide us with a picture of nineteenth-century England that is incomparably vivid, dense, satisfying, and superbly illuminating. The degree of insight into the minute particulars of the actualities of American society in the same period to be gleaned from the pages of Cooper, Hawthorne, Melville, and Twain is infinitely less. Even Henry James, so often regarded as a novelist very much within the English tradition, has less to offer in this connexion than perhaps he seems to. James is always centrally concerned with human behaviour within specific social contexts, and he was undoubtedly an acute observer of both the European and American social scenes. But to compare James with a novelist like Balzac, for whom the representation of an entire society is the keystone of his achievement as a novelist, is to recognize how limited James's range of interest is; how specialized is his concern with society and manners; how American he is in his concern with the ideal society, his conception of what a civilized society ought to be.

Of course American fiction contains many noteworthy examples of the accurate delineation of areas of American society. There is indeed an entire school of American 'realists', including writers such as Dreiser and Dos Passos, or more recently perhaps John Updike or Mary McCarthy, who see themselves as committed exactly to the meticulous rendering of the realities of America. Nevertheless the tradition of the American novel is one of impatience with an exclusive concern with society, with the notion of man as finally a social animal, with any suggestion that society is something fixed and permanent. When society is delineated with careful accuracy in American fiction the intention behind the delineation is almost always one of exposure, of the revelation of the wrongs and injustices that society is perpetrating or encouraging. In any event the English reader who expects to find in American fiction a precise parallel to the social orientation characteristic of the English novel will often be disappointed. Perhaps the American novel in the nineteenth century at least would have been so much the richer had it shown more inclination to come to terms with the actualities of American life. But for its failure to do so there are compensations. Their nature brings us back to the American novel's metaphysical bent.

Writing once of Nathaniel Hawthorne, Anthony Trollope, that exemplary Victorian novelist, acknowledged that 'the creations of American literature are no doubt more given to the speculative, – less given to the realistic, – than are those of English literature. On our side of the water we deal more with beef and ale, and less with dreams.' Trollope's comment is both witty and, in its summary way, accurate. Where the English novel is expansive, wide in its range, seeing the significance of action and behaviour in terms of a relatively stable social morality, the American novel is speculative, enquiring, searching, concerned with the exploration of the meaning of experience in terms of any conceivable value system. Two examples will help to clarify the distinction. Illegitimacy is a common enough theme in nineteenth-century English fiction. It recurs because it is inherently dramatic, capable of bringing an established social position crashing down. Illegitimacy is social dynamite: social ostracism and social ruin are what it implies, as readers of say *Bleak House*, or *Henry Esmond*, or *Daniel Deronda*, will remember. In Melville's *Pierre*, on the other hand, a confused and tortured novel nevertheless written under the same urgent imaginative pressures which had just produced *Moby Dick*, themes of illegitimacy and incest become the springboard for desperate questionings of the nature of human experience and of reality itself. The social issue dissolves almost instantaneously into the metaphysical one. *Pierre* is a novel of the mid-nineteenth century; *The Great Gatsby* was written in the nineteen twenties. But in Fitzgerald's novel too, the social question, which we might expect to be crucial, hardly rises at all. Gatsby's money is made illegally; he is a 'crook', a big-time bootlegger, or something of the sort. Yet Fitzgerald hardly seems to be aware of a problem here: we are invited to admire Gatsby, appreciate his peculiar 'greatness', not dismiss him as morally corrupt. Of course our admiration is not supposed to be uncritical; but the error in Gatsby we are asked to recognize is his innocence, his inability to accept reality as it is, his flawed idealism. His moral and social corruption is disregarded. One could cite still more recent examples: say how in the novels of Bernard Malamud the exploration of the meaning of Jewishness is much less concerned with the place of the Jew in any social context than with ultimate questions about human suffering and the human spirit. But the essential point is the same: as compared with its English counterpart, the American novel is less concerned with a reality defined in primarily social terms, more concerned with metaphysical questionings and searchings.

The distinctive features of American fiction which I have so far described, its preoccupation with the idea of America, its related metaphysical bent, its uncommitted stance in relation to society, have all been ultimately questions of subject-matter. But different subject-matters demand different forms and in fact the forms of the most interesting American fiction are rarely identical with those of English fiction. Once again only dissatisfaction will result if our expectations of the formal aspects of the American novel are simply a carry-over from our experience and knowledge of English fiction.

Of course it is true that there is a large body of American literature, fiction, drama, and poetry, which copies established English models: sentimental novels, decadent romantic verse, and plays of the costume drama kind. The forms of all of these are the forms of their models. But significant American litera-

K

ture is nearly always *formally* interesting: what it says is interesting but *how* it says it is equally so. Consider the poetry of Walt Whitman: rough, crude, long-winded, brash, it is all of these. But it has uninhibited energy and drive, and the way in which it releases that energy and drive has much to do with the way it abandons conventional poetic forms of metre, stanza, rhyme and the rest. Whitman's 'barbaric yawp' demanded a new formal structure for verse, and this at least it achieves. Contemporaneously with Whitman, Emily Dickinson was writing her series of short, lyrical poems, distinguished by a tightness of structure, and economy of language, that has nothing at all in common with the mainstream of English poetry in the nineteenth century. In the twentieth century, American poetry in the hands of Eliot, Pound and Wallace Stevens, and through William Carlos Williams to the Black Mountain poets and the so-called 'confessional' poetry of today, has remained boldly exploratory and experimental in its formal aspect.

One would like to be able to point to examples of nineteenth-century American drama that similarly reveal new strengths, new creative impulses, by a readiness to depart from conventional dramatic forms. Regrettably one cannot. American drama of the nineteenth century has little or nothing to offer the modern reader or theatre-goer. But what is wrong with it is precisely its failure to break free of conventional expression of an equally conventional subject-matter. In the present century the necessary release was achieved. Under the influence of European dramatic movements such as Ibsenesque realism and German expressionism American dramatists finally began to experiment with new dramatic forms capable of giving new life to the American stage. Eugene O'Neill pre-eminently, and more recent dramatists such as Miller and Albee, have explored a considerable range of dramatic modes with enough success to make American drama a substantial reality.

But it is in the novel in particular that the American literary imagination has engaged in the search for new forms and new methods appropriate to the expression of its deepest concerns. The novels of Cooper, the earliest American novelist to command our attention, allow us to see why American fiction of a serious nature was almost compelled to interest itself in the question of the form of the novel. Cooper expressed no interest in problems of literary procedure or technique. He recognized no difficulty in writing American novels other than that of making American manners and scenes interesting to readers accustomed to English manners and scenes. Hence he felt it perfectly proper simply to transfer the essential properties of the romantic, sentimental English novel to an American setting, even to the frontier wilderness itself. Which is exactly what is wrong with his novels. Gentlemen in disguise, damsels in distress, romantic entanglements – these (major) elements of Cooper's novels are now merely tedious distractions from what was his true subject: the recreation of the American wilderness, the problematic frontier society, its authentic inhabitants, and the complex problems of social order and individual liberty arising from the collision of man and nature in the frontier context. In other words Cooper failed to find a fictional form adequate to the fullest exploration of his imaginative vision of America.

Hawthorne, on the other hand, abandoned the novel form altogether. Like Scott, Hawthorne equated the novel with realism. According to this view, the novel is committed to the actual; it portrays an essentially recognizable, familiar world, with verisimilitude as its major virtue. (This is the view of the novel probably shared by the majority of English readers.) For a variety of reasons Hawthorne was unwilling to attempt a realistic recreation of American society or life. Probably, like Cooper before him and James after him, he felt that the realities of American society and life were not sufficiently interesting. Therefore rather than novels Hawthorne writes 'romances'. The romance provides him with the freedom the novel denies him. In the romance form the ideal, the symbolic, the supernatural, are as appropriate as the actual. Hawthorne's novels then tend towards the fabulous, the allegorical and symbolical. If they are to be read at all they demand a kind of attention different to that appropriate to the novel as we perhaps normally understand it. Those moral and psychological themes concerned with guilt and evil, the meaning of the past, idealism and fanaticism, the *rôle* of art and the artist, which preoccupied Hawthorne, are thus expressed through subtle narrative procedures, static, tableau-like scenes, elaborate allegories and symbolisms, and other poetic modes.

In the novels of Melville the search for an appropriate form is even more obsessive. In Melville's fiction the traditional notion of the novel is placed under such severe strains that it constantly collapses. Travelogue, romance, allegory, autobiography (both literal and spiritual), the novel is compelled to encompass each or all of these. Perhaps it is hardly surprising that an early English reviewer of *Moby Dick* described the book as 'maniacal, – mad as a march hare – mowing, gibbering, screaming, like an incurable Bedlamite, reckless of keeper or straight waistcoat'. If we remember the novel's combination of comic realism, uninhibited rhetorical hyperbole and extravagance, superb poetic lyricism, Shakespearean soliloquizing, and other pseudo-dramatic effects, its sections of tremendous narrative speed and energy, and its sardonic, long-winded, satirical meditations, such a view becomes perfectly understandable. The English novel was never like this; the established categories simply do not fit, and the reader's expectations are challenged accordingly.

Even in the novels of Henry James, that supreme master of the art of fiction, the American preoccupation with the problems of form is paramount. James's concern with the way a story is told, his experiments with the varieties of possible narrative methods, with as he put it, 'the story of the story', reflect a sense of the need to make the most of the potential of the novel form, make it more adequate to the strictest aesthetic demand placed upon it. Admittedly, in the twentieth century the major developments in the forms of fiction have been European rather than American in origin: in such a connexion one thinks immediately of Joyce or Proust or the French *nouveau roman*. But American fiction in the same period has been alert to such developments, and has certainly retained its own concern for the possibility of experiment and change in the form of the novel. Take, for example, Dos Passos's quite radical formal experiments in *U.S.A.*; Faulkner's complex use of scrambled chronology, stream of consciousness, mythic parallel and allusion; American attempts to break down the sharp distinction between the novel on the one hand and the collection of short stories on the other; and more recently still attempts, more often than not no doubt unsuccessful, to invent or discover a form for the novel commensurate with the vision of man and society as essentially absurd or disintegrated. One may reasonably conclude that the question of form emerges as one of the most challenging and even disturbing aspects of American literature for the English reader. Henry James always believed that a certain openness towards the chances of experience was a necessary precondition for living the fullest and richest kind of life. A stance of a somewhat similar kind – and James did not believe that openness was finally incompatible with the exercise of a discriminating intelligence – is demanded of us if we are to respond adequately to what American literature has to offer.

In terms of subject-matter and form, then, American literature has much to offer that is interesting, different, and challenging. Subject-matter and form might be seen as composing the basic structures out of which a literature is created. But in a third, still more fundamental area, American literature differs significantly from English literature: in the area of language itself. Paradoxically language is at once the great uniting and disseverating element in the Anglo-American literary situation. The question is not one of the existence of an American language in strict linguistic terms. Rather it is of the literary consequences of the differences between *spoken* English in England and America, and even more, of differing attitudes towards the uses of language in the literary traditions of the two countries.

In early American writing the note of spoken American English is conspicuously absent. Nor is it difficult to understand why. The emphasis of the so-called 'genteel' tradition in American culture in the nineteenth century was hostile to the development of a native American literary style. Probably under the influence of the eighteenth-century Scottish rhetoricians its concern was to encourage the development of a literary style characterized by smoothness, elegance, polish, and correctness. Hence American vernacular speech was ignored. In the work of Hawthorne such a genteel prose is seen at its best. With Melville there is the suggestion of a change: a move towards a rougher, more robust and varied literary language. But the major change comes with Mark Twain. By writing *Huckleberry Finn* Twain demonstrated that the vernacular idioms of American speech could be used to form a sophisticated literary medium not at all incompatible with the kinds of demand that the creative literary imagination places upon language. So it is that Hemingway can assert that all of American literature derived from a single book by Mark Twain called *Huckleberry Finn*. Hemingway exaggerates of course, but it is true that if the language of American literature has often tended to lose something in terms of polish and precision, it has frequently retained a vernacular freshness and toughness, a racy, energetic sinuousness catching something of the vitality of a spoken language. There is no American counterpart to the rather neutral English middle style which most writers largely share – or can often only escape by going 'regional' or 'working-class'. (Perhaps the fact that linguistic differences have always played a crucial part in the English class structure, while they have never done so in America, is a clue to the source of the literary distinction I am trying to make.) Of course I am not suggesting that the literary languages of England and America are strictly uniform – not even in their differences. But American literature rarely sounds quite like English literature; and in trying to say why one comes back to the notion that in comparison with the language of English literature that of American literature is less 'literary', a shade closer to the spoken vernacular, and certainly more varied.

The variety is a consequence of a different attitude within the American literary tradition to the possibilities of language. How the word 'rhetorical' is used is a useful shorthand for indicating the nature of this final distinction. When an English critic describes an author's style as 'rhetorical' it is difficult not to feel that a faintly adverse comment has been made. For most of us 'rhetorical' has come to be associated with notions of over-writing, of lack of precision, perhaps of linguistic extravagance or even a kind of verbal self-indulgence. Yet a rhetorical uninhibitedness is often highly characteristic of American writing. Writers as diverse as Henry James and Faulkner, or Walt Whitman and Wallace Stevens, frequently use a rhetorical style that may strike the English reader as inflated and extreme, or even extravagant and bizarre. Here again of course there is no question of absolute statements. Not all American writing is highly rhetorical. American authors are perfectly capable, on occasion, of writing in a tight, terse, economical style: the example of Hemingway, for example, makes that abundantly clear. But it is none the less true that the American literary tradition smiles on a use of language that is often no doubt dangerously uninhibited, free-ranging, and exploratory. Risking much, it sometimes falls flat; rhetorical expansiveness can easily become a pretentious, high-sounding nonsense. Equally an elaborate and complex rhetoric can often be the appropriate mode of expression for an intensely creative literary imagination. (More interesting still, perhaps, is the way in which some American authors seem to have two distinct styles at their command: one all economy, tautness, precision; the other loose, free-flowing, unstructured. Compare, for example, Saul Bellow's style in *Dangling Man* or *The Victim* with that of his later novels, *The Adventures of Angie March* or *Henderson the Rain-King*; or William Styron's style in the novella *The Long March* with that of his full-scale novels; or even Faulkner's style in the hunting sections of *The Bear* with that of the long meditative sections.)

In subject-matter, in form, in language itself – in all of these primary dimensions of the work of literature – American literature offers much that is distinctive, urgent, and original. It is a literature which fails perhaps as often as it succeeds; a literature which echoes much of the restlessness, the endlessly enquiring, soul-searching quality of America itself. Certainly it is a literature that raises many more issues and many more questions than it manages to resolve. But it is not a complacent or self-satisfied literature. Somewhere on the long, familiar road from *Beowulf* to Virginia Woolf take at least a stroll down the New World turning. Hopefully you will return to the main highway, enlivened and refreshed by a new and valuable literary experience.

# 8

---

# Literature and Psychology

*Laurence Lerner*

The first thing to say is that English universities do not offer the chance to study these two subjects together. At universities which offer general degrees, in which you choose a number of different subjects from a long list, it is of course possible to choose both English literature and psychology; but the connexions between them will be left to the student himself. A surprising number of academic psychologists started their careers with literary degrees, and a lot of literary critics are interested in psycho-analysis. But I do not know any British university in which undergraduates can study the interrelations between these disciplines in the form of a dialogue between literary men and psychologists. The University of Sussex offers this in a seminar for its graduate students, but not for undergraduates. Largely this difficulty comes from the way universities are organized, and from the sort of context in which each of these subjects is studied. Psychology belongs among the social sciences, and the studies that usually accompany it are sociology, physiology, statistics and clinical observations: it is hardly ever studied historically. English literature belongs among the humanities, and is accompanied by a foreign language and its literature, or history, or philosophy.

Yet both literature and psychology are a study of man. The differences of approach are enormous, but the subject-matter is theoretically identical. A novelist is an uncertificated expert on human behaviour. The psychologist's field is human behaviour – and that clearly includes the writing, reading and discussing of poems and plays. It is hard to believe that the subjects do not overlap, and that the practitioners of each have nothing to teach each other. The aim of this article is to suggest, and briefly explore, some of the overlaps.

**Projection tests and artistic creation**

The concept of projection is part of psycho-analytic theory. It is the tendency to attribute to other people feelings and wishes that we have repressed in ourselves; and it forms one of the defence mechanisms by which, according to psycho-analysis, those contents of the unconscious which threaten us are kept out of consciousness. The husband who feels unconscious hostility to his wife believes – and says – that she is hostile to him. The prudish old maid sees – and disapproves of – sexual insinuations all round her; this is because of the strength of her own repressed erotic impulses. There is some evidence for the existence of the mechanism of projection, and it is clear that as it operates it will distort our picture of the world. When this reaches the point of neurosis, we have lost all sense of reality: the outside world is simply a reflection of our anxieties. Normal people – this is one definition of normality – are able to resist these distortions: their perception of reality is stronger than their projections. But it is a central belief of psycho-analysis that the mechanisms which make us mentally ill are present in everyone; the neurotic is simply the man or woman in whom they have got out of hand, and rendered him unable to cope with the practical tasks of living. Neurotic and normal differ only in degree, or, as Freud said, 'we are all ill'.

If we could find out how a man's picture of the world is distorted, we would then know what his unconscious fears and wishes are. This information would be useful clinically, if we needed to cure his neurosis, or for research, if we wanted to study his personality and compare it with others. But to sort out the distortions from a true version of his world might be very difficult: if for instance we ask him to describe the members of his family, we would need to undertake a long study of what they were actually like before we could spot where he had misrepresented them – and how could we ever be sure that we were right and he was wrong? In order to study projection, therefore, we must present people with something so vague and general that everything they say about it will come from them, not from it; and at the same time so stimulating that they will be led to say a good bit about it.

'Do you see yonder cloud,' said Hamlet to Polonius, 'that's almost in the shape of a camel?'

| | |
|---|---|
| *Polonius* | By th'mass, and 'tis, like a camel indeed. |
| *Hamlet* | Methinks it is like a weasel. |
| *Polonius* | It is backed like a weasel. |
| *Hamlet* | Or like a whale? |
| *Polonius* | Very like a whale. |

The cloud looks very like whatever you choose to see in it. Hamlet was setting himself a projection test (no doubt the first ever). The fact that he kept seeing animals would interest a psychologist who was trying to study his personality. 'The animal kingdom is within the field of experience of virtually every subject . . . The more a subject is able to choose his concepts outside this most obvious area, the less likely he is to be confined to the obvious, the stereotyped, or a narrow range of interests.' What a sad conclusion this suggests about Hamlet's personality: if all he could see was animals, he was bound by stereotypes (unless of course he was simply describing what he expected Polonius to see!).

A cloud is ideal material for a projection test – or would be if it would keep still. But because clouds keep changing, psychologists use inkblots instead. The Rorschach inkblot test was devised by a Swiss psychologist in 1911, and has now become the most widely used of projection tests. The subject is shown a series of ten standardized inkblots, and asked to describe what he sees in them. His responses are 'scored' in a most elaborate way, according to location (does he use the whole blot, large or small, usual or unusual details), determinants (does he use movement, form, colour or chiaroscuro) and content (does he see human figures, human details, animals, man-made objects, etc.). The total scores, the fractions and the ratios between the different factors are elaborately calculated, and then comes the controversial part, the interpretation. One detail, on animal interpretation, has already been quoted, from Klopfer and Kelly's manual *The Rorschach Technique*. I cannot here describe the very complicated interpretative procedure. The ratio between the number of whole figure responses and the number of movement-determinants, for instance, is 'an intra-individual ratio which . . . can be used as an indicator . . . for the relationship between drive for intellectual conquest and personal productive capacity to make these conquests substantial'. Or the response to colour (some of the blots are in two or more colours) is considered an indication of our emotional response to the outside world: thus a subject who 'refuses . . . to acknowledge any influence of colour on his responses certainly evidences an extreme reticence towards emotional entanglements'.

There are obvious objections to the Rorschach test. Because it is a test of perception, the answers it produces refer to the actual world, and it is only a deduction that they really come from the subject's personality. And as we have seen, these answers are not a direct revelation of that personality, but need a good deal of interpreting, often questionable interpreting. To counter these objections, psychologists have devised what they call an apperception, not a perception test – one in which the stimulus simply sets you going, and the answer comes from your fantasy. It is quite useless to ask the subjects what they are thinking and dreaming about, since they will then *inspect* their own minds, and will give us a conscious answer. We must fix their attention on something outside themselves, but they must not talk about that. How is this to be done?

The answer is easy: we get them to tell us a story. There are several variations of this test, the Thematic Apperception Test (TAT), but they are all similar in outline. We show the subject a series of pictures, as general as we can manage: a man covering his face with his hands, with behind him a woman in bed; a young boy looking intently at a violin; a grief-stricken figure of uncertain sex. Or perhaps we start a story, in very general terms, and ask him to continue. The stories which different subjects tell vary enormously: and since they all began from the same picture, the differences must spring from the subjects themselves. If there is a man and a woman in the picture, you can identify with either; you can suggest hostility, love or estrangement between them; you can insert a mother-figure in the story, or a father-figure, or a child; the father can be strong or weak, benevolent or hostile; the ending can be happy or unhappy . . .

Now such subjects are not the only ones who tell stories; and we must naturally be anxious to know if the TAT can tell us anything about story-telling, or the Rorschach anything about shapes. What subjects are being asked is to be artists – not because we want the products as works of art, but because the process is thought to be revealing. Do real artists go through the same process?

According to psycho-analytic theory, they do. Freud often liked to point out that art, being based on fantasy, was closely linked to the unconscious. 'The artist is originally a man who turns from reality because he cannot come to terms with the demand for the renunciation of instinctual satisfaction as it is first made, and who then in phantasy-life allows full play to his erotic and ambitious wishes.' Fantasy (which includes day-dreaming) offers us a substitute gratification of our unconscious wishes; and the artist, according to Freud, is a man of peculiarly intense fantasy-life, and has a mysterious power of expressing it in such a way that it appeals to the fantasies of others. The drawings of Toulouse-Lautrec are famed for their nervous strength of line, their marvellous rendering of graceful movement, in dancers, jockeys, circus performers. Toulouse-Lautrec himself was a cripple, and the drawings must therefore enact what he was longing to do but couldn't. In this case, the impossibility was physical and the wish conscious; the profounder and more typical origin of art, for Freud, lies in unconscious wishes which could not be formulated because they are forbidden, and which must therefore be expressed symbolically. By asking the subject of the TAT to tell a story about the picture we offer some sort of disguise for his material: his stories can tell of young men shooting old men, or of cruel old men acting as tyrants, and he need not realize that he is displaying hostility to his father.

Let us imagine Charles Dickens or Marcel Proust being given the TAT. They would both, we may be sure, write a lot. Dickens might see the children as cruelly treated by sternly moral parents, put out to work before they had finished their schooling, frightened by cruel and ugly adults. Proust might see the young men as sensitive and ineffectual, living more in fantasy than reality, obsessed by homosexual temptations. In this way they might offer the psychologist an unprecedentedly rich revelation of themselves. But as they wrote, other factors might enter in. Dickens might remember several glorious malapropisms he had heard recently, and after a moment's thought might combine them very effectively into one very funny sentence. Proust might decide it was prudent to recast the homosexual story as a heterosexual one. Dickens might decide that he'd told too many stories about neglected children, and tell one in which the parents were well-meaning and the child ungrateful. Proust might see the boy with the violin, think of a friend who was a violinist, and tell the story of something the friend had done, straightforwardly and unadorned. Dickens might decide to make life interesting for the psychologist by putting in a little suspense . . . And the result might be unprecedentedly misleading as self-revelation.

How far is the novelist a man who writes out his own unconscious fantasies? Are his novels an extreme case of what the TAT is looking for, or are they more like the opposite? The question is not easy, and the answer has to be complicated. For a great novelist is both more inspired and more competent than the psychologist's subjects. More inspired – this means, nowadays, that he has more access to the sources of power in his unconscious, so that his work will be charged with power by his own obsessive emotional concerns: to this extent, he will be a splendid subject for TAT. But more competent, too – able, that is, to modify his material according to other, conscious criteria, such as shrewd observation and reproducing what he sees and hears; or knowing how to please or excite his readers; or how to write elegantly, avoid monotony, make us laugh.

## Unconscious intentions

Adrian Leverkühn, the hero of Thomas Mann's novel *Dr Faustus*, is a composer of genius who lives the life of a recluse in a village near Munich, loved but never quite understood by his few friends. He makes one attempt to get married. When he is about 40, he asks his friend Rudi Schwerdtfenger to propose on his behalf to a Frenchwoman they have recently met, called Marie Godeau. Rudi confesses in reply that he himself loves Marie. After a moment's hesitation, Adrian repeats the request: it will be a sacrifice, and Rudi, who loves him, may want to make such a sacrifice. Schwerdtfenger's behaviour is honourable. He delivers the proposal conscientiously, and only after Marie (deeply offended) has replied that she would never marry Adrian, does he woo for himself, and after some resistance succeeds. This destroys his friendship with Adrian, and because of the complications of his own life causes his tragic death.

Clarissa Harlowe, heroine of Richardson's novel *Clarissa*, is, when the story opens, being forced by her family to marry the repulsive Solmes for his property; and finds that the only way of escape seems to be through the handsome rake Lovelace, who is interested in her and hated by her family. Writing to her friend Anna Howe, Clarissa says that what liking she feels for him, 'is owing more to the usage he has received, and for my sake borne, than to any personal consideration'. Anna's reply is shrewd and teasing: 'depend upon it, whether you know it or not, you are a little in for't'. She believes that Clarissa is falling in love with Lovelace, and that he knows this: 'he has seen more than *I* have seen, more than you think *could* be seen; more than you *yourself* know'. Nothing in the subsequent action of the book confirms Anna's diagnosis, yet there are continual suggestions of a hidden shame in Clarissa, of motives not fully understood, of a bond between her and Lovelace that the facts can't altogether explain.

Both these episodes can be described in psycho-analytic terms. Why did Adrian ask his friend to woo for him? 'Could he have seriously conceived the idea,' asks Mann's narrator, 'that what Rudolf "gave out" – in other words the young man's undeniable sexual appeal – could be made to work and woo for him, Adrian?' Such appeal is as likely to be dangerous as helpful; and a much more acceptable explanation is that Adrian unconsciously feared marriage and the loss of his freedom, and therefore sent his proposal in a way that would lead to its rejection. And why Rudi? There are hints in the novel of a homosexual element in their affection for each other, and if Adrian's fear of marriage was sexual, then Rudi was the right man to choose.

Schwerdtfenger too may have been influenced by unconscious motives. He may have resented a cooling that he detected in Adrian's feelings for him, and the fact that he was being used as an instrument. 'I believe,' says the narrator, 'that in his heart he now felt free', and though he is scrupulous in carrying out his promise he may well have used his own charm to undermine rather than to reinforce the case he pleaded to Marie. And then finally there are hints of some even deeper motivation from Adrian, of a peculiarly horrible kind, 'harsher, colder, crueller than my good nature would have been capable of without stiffening in icy horror'. This must refer to a hidden wish to kill his friend, the friend who had courted his affection for so many years, for whom he had recently written a violin concerto, and towards whom he must then have felt a profound unconscious resentment.

We could not say any of this without the vocabulary and concepts of psycho-analysis, without the idea of unconscious motivation, or the view that we also hate those we love, and that affection may be purchased by the repression of hostility. In the case of *Clarissa*, we can of course sum up Anna Howe's view by saying that Clarissa, from the beginning, was unconsciously in love with Lovelace; and see the unfolding of the story as a slow revelation to her of her own feelings, so that her final death is caused not simply by horror at what was done to her, but by shame at her own hidden responsibility for it. If we interpret the novel in this way, then Clarissa's dream, in which Lovelace 'stabbed me to the heart, and then tumbled me into a deep grave . . . throwing in the dirt and earth upon me with his hands' becomes a vivid representation of her unconscious sexual fears, and a prophecy of what happens to her, not a supernatural but a psychological prophecy.

Here are two novels, almost exactly two hundred years apart, whose action can be described in psycho-analytic terms. What is the point of doing this? Any interpretation of a novel needs terminology rather more abstract than that used in the story, so that it can say, here is the point about human behaviour that is being made; and any terms that fit are therefore useful. If the terms belong to some wider context of systematic theory, then they have the advantage that they help us to place that novel – or the novel as a whole – in that context. How useful *this* is depends on what you think of psycho-analysis.

Of course there is one obvious difference between the two. We know that Thomas Mann had read Freud; and even if he hadn't, any novelist writing in 1945 must have picked up a good deal of the ideas of psycho-analysis. But what did Richardson know of repressed sexual fears, or of dreams as the fulfilment of unconscious wishes, or anxiety wishes? What is the difference between psycho-analytic interpretations of pre- and post-Freudian works?

There seem to be three possible answers to this: that it makes no difference; or that it is more appropriate for pre-Freudian works; or for modern works. The committed Freudian is likely to give the first answer. If Freud's achievement was to uncover psychic mechanisms that we have always used; if he was right in his own famous claim that the great poets and philosophers had discovered the unconscious long before him, and his contribution had simply been to study it scientifically; then there is nothing surprising in finding Freudian ideas used as the basis of a novel published in 1747. The novelist may have known nothing of the theories, but his own unconscious could have led him to many of the insights. Novelists write, as human beings act, from deeper sources than the intellect; whether a novelist has come across a particular theory in his reading is of only superficial importance: the true shape of his books comes from his own unconscious fears and wishes, and the insights these have led him to. This will apply equally to the present and the past, so the difference between knowing and not knowing psycho-analytic theory is unimportant.

In contrast to this is the view that Freudian interpretations fit post-Freudian literature, in the same way that neo-Platonic interpretations fit Spenser, or the theory of humours fits Ben Jonson. A writer uses the intellectual apparatus of his time. Mann therefore used psycho-analysis, and to see what point he is making about Adrian and Rudi we shall naturally find it helpful to read Freud. But to understand Richardson's view of human nature we ought to read Shaftesbury or Locke or Horace or whoever he (or his friends) had read. This view is as far as can be from the Freudian's: it is not interested in the truth of psycho-analysis, but treats it simply as part of the history of ideas. It assumes that the theories a novelist holds, not the shape of his emotional life, determine the structure of his books.

Somewhere between these two is the view that perhaps seems

ridiculous at first glance, that psycho-analysis is more help with pre- than with post-Freudian literature. This view supposes a partial allegiance to Freud. It believes that writers can sense the shape of theories that no one has yet formulated; that the symbols of a poem can express – and evoke – elements in our unconscious, and derive their power from this emotional charge. But it also believes that too much theory can interfere with this. Now that psycho-analysis can be learned from books, it is too easy for the novelist to use it: he may scatter his work with symbols that he has laboriously worked out, and it may be hard for us to sort out the genuine (coming from the unconscious) and the fake. This view differs from the second in that it regards the unconscious as an important discovery, and gives a real, not merely a historical, significance to a novelist's use of it; but it fears (whereas the first view dismisses) the discoveries that a novelist has not made for himself.

What we might call a subdivision of this view claims that the late nineteenth century (the time when Freud was making his discoveries) was a uniquely valuable moment for the novelist: a time when intellectual influences were converging towards the concept of the dynamic unconscious, but when it was still beneath the surface, so that great sensitivity to human problems might lead a writer gropingly towards it – a time when such a discovery was possible but had to be made the hard way.

One final point concerns the way in which awareness of the unconscious manifests itself in the work. In *Dr Faustus*, a highly self-conscious novel, there is some explicit discussion of Adrian's unconscious motives, and this is hardly conceivable before Freud. In pre-Freudian work such awareness will take symbolic rather than explicit form – dreams, images, or even the development of the plot. There is a place for both in fiction, but it is the second kind that is peculiar to literature.

## Behaviourism

In all I have so far said, I have taken 'psychology' to mean 'psycho-analysis'; and it is certainly true that both writers and critics with psychological interests have tended to take their psychology from Freud and his followers. This is understand-

able: psycho-analysis is the boldest school of modern psychology, the one with the most complex and ambitious theories of
motivation, the one which has not hesitated to describe the
topography and functioning of the whole personality. Freud
had little scientific caution when he devised theories, and they
are theories of the whole man. The literary man, educated in
a humanist tradition, is likely to grow impatient with experimental psychologists who study eye-movements in reading, or
measure how many tenths of a second it takes to react to a
stimulus; and to feel that the psycho-analyst, like himself,
shows a bold interest in understanding man, not a patient
attempt to accumulate little bricks of knowledge.

All the same, it is true that many modern psychologists are
sceptical of psycho-analysis; and if we are really interested in
psychology, and prepared to study it on its own terms, we must
think about behaviourism, the rival philosophy that has
directed so much experimental work in this century. Students
of literature are not likely to care much about particular, detailed experiments on eye-movements, pulse-rates or colour
vision (though some of the more colourful experiments on
aggression or development, done on humans or monkeys, make
wonderful subjects for poems?). Our concern will be with the
view of man that underlies behaviourism, and we must allow
behaviourists to state this for themselves.

> States of consciousness like the so-called phenomena of
> spiritualism are not objectively verifiable, and for that reason
> never become data for science . . . The behaviourist finds no
> evidence for 'mental existences' or 'mental processes' of any
> kind.

That statement is by J. B. Watson, the founder and the
extremist of behaviourism. Impatient with the kind of psychology that asked subjects to describe their feelings, because it
seemed impossible to check the results, or be sure that two
subjects meant the same when they claimed to feel 'elated', or
to have 'mixed feelings', he proposed to dismiss all mental
concepts as fictions, and study only what can be observed and
checked. A latter-day behaviourist, B. F. Skinner, states much
the same position:

When we describe people as exercising qualities of mind, we are not referring to occult experiences of which their overt acts and utterances are effects; we are referring to those overt acts and utterances themselves.

Most experimental psychologists nowadays are behaviourists. Either they are methodological behaviourists ('mental agnostics', let us say) who believe in omitting from psychology all concepts that cannot be described in operant terms, i.e. in terms of observable and checkable behaviour, and in studying only what can be studied by strictly scientific methods; or else they are dogmatic behaviourists ('mental atheists') who deny the existence of the mind, the unconscious, the repressed wish, even the wish, as 'fictions'. D. E. Broadbent sums up the position of the modern behaviourist: it entails

> rejecting concepts which are not defined by any operation; rejecting a man's statements about his experience unless his words have been given some unambiguous meaning. So we reach the view of science which relates events at the bodily senses ('stimuli') to events at those parts of the body which act on the outer world ('responses').

Instead of talking about fear and guilt, fancy and imagination, impulse or meditation, we should talk about environment and behaviour: known stimuli and observable responses. Can all this possibly have any literary interest?

In Book V of Dostoyevsky's *The Brothers Karamazov* Fyodor tries to persuade his son Ivan to go to a near-by town to do business for him. A merchant called Gorstkin has offered him 11,000 roubles for a copse he owns, and he wants Ivan to find out whether Gorstkin, whom he considers a rogue, is lying or speaking the truth. He then advises Ivan how to do this:

> 'What you have to find out is whether he is lying or speaking the truth, when he says he wants to buy it and would give eleven thousand.'
> 'I shall be no use in such a business. I have no eye either.'
> 'Stay, wait a bit! You will be of use, for I will tell you the signs by which you can judge about Gorstkin. I've done business with him a long time. You see, you must watch his beard; he has a nasty, thin, red beard. If his head shakes

when he talks and he gets cross, it's all right, he is saying what he means, he wants to do business. But if he strokes his beard with his left hand and grins – he is trying to cheat you. Don't watch his eyes, you won't find out anything from his eyes, he is a deep one, a rogue – but watch his beard!'

This is pure behaviourism. Fyodor, like a good psychologist, has conducted experiments. He has watched Gorstkin when doing business with him, and has found that when his beard shakes he does business on the lines he has offered; when he strokes it, he doesn't. Having observed this connexion, he is now able to make predictions. It is true that Fyodor describes his discovery in 'mentalist' terms – 'He is saying what he means' – but it would be easy to turn these into the 'operant' terms of a behaviourist, for what he is really concerned to discover is what Gorstkin will *do*. We could easily rephrase Fyodor's points in the unimpeachable language of the experimentalist: there is a high correlation between the shaking of Gorstkin's beard and his actually purchasing goods for more or less the price he has named; and a low correlation of that with beard-stroking.

A shrewd businessman, we can conclude, he needs to be a good behaviourist; so does a novelist. The novelists we trust are those who *see* their characters, and report their behaviour convincingly – George Eliot, for example, who describes Gwendolen Grandcourt calling on Mirah to find out if a rumour about Daniel Deronda is true – a rumour that has greatly upset her. She

began to unbutton her gloves that she might button them again, and bite her lips over the pretended difficulty.

Here is a less obvious example, from a very different novelist:

Karl could not detect any malice in these words; the bad news which had lain sheathed in Green the whole evening was delivered, and now he seemed a harmless man with whom one could speak more frankly perhaps, than with anybody else. The best of men, chosen through no fault of his own to be the bearer of such a secret and painful message, must appear a suspicious character so long as he had to keep it to himself (Franz Kafka, *America*, Ch. III).

Here too there are a good many mentalist terms ('malice', 'suspicious', 'fault' – though the last is really part of a digression in Karl's mind); all the same, the passage is an observation of behaviour. The man who had bad news to deliver shows this in the way he talks, and will, once it is uttered, talk differently and less aggressively.

Now if we compare not only these two examples, but the two novelists, we can notice that whereas the first is typical, the second isn't. George Eliot is full of such touches of observation: how Mr Tulliver sat on his horse, how Celia dressed, how Mr Casaubon spoke. Her marvellous eye missed nothing. But Kafka's novels take place in a world that is only half-real. Everyone's behaviour is unpredictable: just as we (and the hero) are beginning to make sense of it, it begins to look totally irrational. The commonest emotion of the hero is frustration; and those aspects of the environment that are most convincingly rendered are those that frustrate – telephones where the man at the other end goes away or gets inaudible, clerks who give unwanted information and evade our questions. It is a highly selective, distorted picture of the world.

The usual way to describe the difference is to call George Eliot a realist, Kafka a symbolic novelist. 'How little the real characteristics of the working-classes are known to those outside,' complained George Eliot in her essay on Riehl,

is sufficiently disclosed by our Art as well as by our political and social theories. Where, in our picture exhibitions, shall we find a group of true peasantry?

Even the most truthful of our painters, she complains later,

treat their subjects under the influence of traditions and prepossessions rather than of direct observation.

To set against this, let us take not a theoretic pronouncement by Kafka, but an extract from his diaries:

In the afternoon while falling asleep. As though the solid skull-cap encircling the insensitive cranium had moved more deeply inwards and left a part of the brain exposed to the free play of light and muscles.

The difference between these two novelists is clearly immense. Kafka shapes his world in response to his obsessions, George Eliot believes in observation and truth. Of course there is external truth in Kafka, as we have seen, but it is only found in details, or in those parts of his world that fit his obsessions. And of course George Eliot's emotions shaped her books, for she is a novelist, not a sociologist, but only through selection, not through distortion. If we think of the general nature of their fictional worlds, the contrast holds.

And it is a contrast with psychological implications. To attend to observable behaviour, to introduce mental concepts only if you can give an operant description of them, is a procedure George Eliot would have understood, even (perhaps) felt attracted to – not because she did not believe there was such a thing as joy or repentance, but because she wanted to know (and show us) how our sentences change their shape when we rejoice, what tricks of the body reveal that we have repented. Out of such reliable elements, Kafka could never have built his brilliantly distorted world. Behaviourism is the psychology for realists.

### Past literature and past psychology

The science of psychology is about a century old. Its founders are generally considered to be Wundt and Helmholtz, Freud, James and Pavlov – all born in the first two thirds of the nineteenth century. But theories about human nature are much older than that: the reason there was no science of psychology before then is that such theories were not tested, they were not hypotheses but dogmas, or speculations. Now the literary man's interest in psychology does not lie in the verification by particular experiments. It is not the *science* of psychology that he cares for, and he may then be almost as interested in past as in present psychology – if he can find it.

Can we study the relations between past literature and past, not present, psychology? In order to find past psychology, we have first to realize that it will be called something else, medicine, for instance, or philosophy, or demonology.

John Locke's *Essay concerning Human Understanding*, first published in 1690, contains a good deal that we would today call psychology. It contains a theory of human motivation that can fairly be called rationalist. The great privilege of being human, that distinguishes men from animals, is 'that they can suspend their desires, and stop them from determining their wills to any action, till they have duly and fairly examined the good and evil of it, as far forth as the weight of the thing requires'. We are able, in other words, to take a long view; to refrain from immediate gratification, and plan. When we act against our own interests, it is because we have not realized the full implications of our actions.

> Were the pains of honest industry and of starving with hunger and cold set together before us, nobody would be in doubt which to choose: were the satisfaction of a lust and the joys of heaven offered at once to any one's present possession, he would not balance, or err in the determination of his choice.

If only we didn't make the mistake of paying more attention to the present than to the future, we would act right; but most men, 'like spendthrift heirs, are apt to judge a little in hand better than a great deal to come'. The cause then of wrong actions is 'the weak and narrow constitution of our minds'. It is clear why we can call this a rationalist theory: it equates wrongdoing with the making of mistakes. It might seem at first that this applies only to acts that harm ourselves; but if you regard Christianity – as Locke evidently does – as a system for keeping us moral by rewarding and punishing us in the next world, then immoral actions are, eventually, against our own interests, vice and folly are the same, and *all* kinds of wrong deeds are due to the weak and narrow constitution of our minds.

This is the opposite to those psycho-analytically influenced theories that see man as a pain-seeking as well as a pleasure-seeking creature, and speak of a psychological 'need for punishment'; or to St Paul's famous utterance, 'I find then a law, that, when I would do good, evil is present with me.' St Paul's 'law' is a positive force, not merely error or lack of foresight.

Locke was widely read and highly thought of in the eighteenth century; most of the novelists had either read him or knew of his theories. Yet it is hard to find a novelist who really believes in Locke's rationalism. Even Fielding, probably the most rationalist of eighteenth-century novelists, does not believe that the virtuous take long views and the vicious have weak and narrow minds. On the contrary, he shows his hero, Tom Jones, to be almost incapable of considering the consequences of his actions, and Blifil, the calculating hypocrite who is contrasted with him, to be much shrewder. Jones is the hero because his impulses are generous; Blifil is the villain because he is interested only in himself, not because he cannot take long views. In fact he is very good at long views; and his eventual defeat is due more to the demands of the plot for a happy ending than to any real plausibility. This rather conventional happy ending is easier to reconcile with Locke than is the portrayal of Jones. And the character with the weakest and narrowest mind is probably Squire Western, who acts entirely on impulse, and swings from one extreme to the other; by Locke's psychology he should be quite incapable of good or wise actions, but Fielding clearly believes that in the midst of his wildest injustices Squire Western has a generous streak, a certain natural warmth, that makes it difficult for us to hate him.

And if we turn to the greatest novel of the eighteenth century, we find ourselves in a world that has virtually no contact with Locke's. Choderlos de Laclos' *Les Liaisons Dangereuses* is a study of the passions of lust, greed and above all love of power that lead its characters to destroy others and, eventually, themselves. The supreme good of the Vicomte de Valmont is power over others. His aim is not only to seduce, but to do so in the most complicated way. 'That was no ordinary trick,' he boasts; or, later, 'behold her, conquered at last, that proud woman who dared to think she could resist me'. The whole of this long, complex novel is an exploration of Valmont's egoism, its intensity, its effect on others, its eventual self-defeat. Compared to such an exploration, how naïve Locke's theory of motivation seems to be. Valmont knows perfectly well what he is doing, and is driven on by the intensity of an egoism that sees quite clearly the nature and consequences of its actions.

The novelists, we conclude, were finer psychologists than the philosophers. Theories of the human heart ignored the complications of reality in a way the story-tellers, with their more intuitive understanding, found it hard to do.

For another example, I turn to poetic drama. The comedies of Ben Jonson are based on the once-famous theory of humours – a theory of personality-types that classified people according to the dominance in their make-up of one of the four humours, choler, melancholy, phlegm and blood. What most interested Jonson in this theory was the idea of the dominant passion, that so possessed a man that it shaped his whole conduct, converting him into a continual embodiment of that one passion. Kitely, for example, the jealous husband in *Every Man in his Humour* is a choleric man, and is unable to think of anything but his jealousy of his wife:

> A New disease? I know not, new or old
> But it may well be called poor mortals Plague;
> For like a pestilence it doth infect
> The houses of the brain: first it begins
> Solely to work upon the Phantasy,
> Filling her seat with such pestiferous air,
> As soon corrupts the judgement, and from thence
> Sends like contagion to the memory,
> Still each of other catching the infection,
> Which as a searching vapour spreads itself
> Confusedly through every sensitive part
> Till not a thought or motion in the mind
> Be free from the black poison of suspect.

This is lively writing, and a vivid representation of the agitations of jealousy – comic yet not merely comic, so that we both laugh at Kitely and also feel there is something real in his emotion. It can be appreciated by the modern reader who knows nothing of the theory of humours; but if we want to relate drama to the ideas that underly it, we will naturally look at that theory, and ask how useful it is to us.

Jonson has written in terms of faculty psychology, that is, he assumes there are separate and identifiable faculties in the mind which can be named and (even) anatomically located. The disease of jealousy acts on them one after the other – on phantasy, judgment, memory. Its effect is described in terms of a comparison with a contagious disease. Thus each faculty has its own house in the brain, from which the infection spreads to the next. Now it may well be that Elizabethan readers took this description more literally than we do. Commentators on Jonson quote sixteenth-century anatomical treatises that indicate how the various virtues, or faculties, are situated each in its own 'ventricle' or 'cell' of the brain. The modern reader, however vividly he enjoys the passage, will never dream of taking 'houses' as a technical term. Probably he will think of all attempts to locate faculties in parts of the brain as simply convenient metaphors. This does not prevent us enjoying the lines, but we may be more sceptical than the Elizabethans (at any rate, than the more pedestrian Elizabethans) about their dependence on contemporary psychological theory.

In contrast, here is a modern poem that also draws on psychological theory:

> Dear, though the night is gone,
> Its dream still haunts today,
> That brought us to a room
> Cavernous, lofty as
> A railway terminus,
> And crowded in that gloom
> Were beds, and we in one
> In a far corner lay.
>
> Our whisper woke no clocks,
> We kissed, and I was glad
> At everything you did,
> Indifferent to those
> Who sat with hostile eyes
> In pairs on every bed,
> Arms round each other's neck,
> Inert and vaguely sad.
>
> O but what worm of guilt
> Or what malignant doubt
> Am I the victim of,
> That you then, unabashed,
> Did what I never wished,
> Confessed another love;
> And I submissive, felt
> Unwanted and went out?
>
>                                   W. H. Auden

This poem uses psycho-analysis. It does so in general, by attributing psychological significance to dreams. The speaker narrates his dream because he believes it to be evidence for parts of his own psyche that he does not know about. And in narrating it, he uses one specific psycho-analytic concept, one we have already mentioned, that of projection. In the dream, the girl unaccountably deserts him; and he interprets this by attributing the 'worm of guilt', the 'doubt', to *himself* – since such doubt, repressed from his own consciousness, will be projected onto her. Without understanding this point, we cannot understand the poem.

Auden's poem depends more closely on psycho-analysis than Jonson's does on humour theory. The question of how literally we take Jonson's terms does not determine whether or not we understand his passage; but Auden has only introduced the main act – you went out – in order to make his point, and if we don't see the point the act will puzzle or mislead.

Does this mean that the value of his poem depends on the truth of the theory? This is hard to answer, for it depends on our view of poetry – how far we regard poems as emotional experiences, how far we believe they offer insights. This poem, since it actually claims to offer an insight, surely must depend on theory more than most – or at least the last stanza must. There is projection in the second stanza too, but in a more general way: the most likely explanation, psychologically, for the hostility of the surrounding couples, 'inert and vaguely sad', is surely a feeling of detachment and vague hostility to his environment in the dreamer, which he has once again attributed to the world around him. But we do not have to know this; it may not even be what the poet meant. And the first stanza is simply based on a general feeling that dreams can be disturbing and important: the huge room has no precise symbolic meaning, it simply corresponds to the speaker's lonely anxiety, in the way any poetic image might correspond to an emotion.

If psycho-analysis is one day rejected as thoroughly as the theory of humours now is, the last stanza of the poem may come to seem pointless, whereas the dream as a whole will still feel disturbing. It is not necessary, if we are to be moved by it, to believe that dreams are the symbolic expressions of unconscious wishes, though we must certainly believe they are expressions of something in us. But then unless they come to us from gods, or are the result of sheer chance, everyone must believe that.

## Conclusion

The purpose of this essay has not been to survey all the possible interrelations between literature and psychology, but to offer some particular problems, and ways of discussing them. It should now be easy to conclude with a few more systematic remarks.

There are two possible relationships between psychologist and poet (or novelist). The poet can be regarded as his subject, or as his colleague. That is, literature can be part of the subject-matter of psychology, which offers us theories on poetic creation, on the relation of fantasy and art, on whether the artist is a neurotic, on the psychological significance of distortions of reality. This will mean that psychologist and literary critic are colleagues, and can lead both to theories of literature in general, and to interpretations of particular works. On both these questions there is much to say that this essay has not been able to touch on. Freud has a theory of art, and there have been more sophisticated and convincing theories than his which still use a Freudian scheme of the mind – those of Kris, Lesser or Kubie for instance. And the unravelling of the unconscious meaning of poetic symbols has become an industry among one school of literary critics. Its validity depends on how far we think poetic symbols should be treated as dream symbols are, that is, as disguises to be stripped away so that the latent content can be revealed. Although Auden's poem is a dream, it certainly does not ask to be treated in that way.

Much less has been written on literature from the viewpoint that sees poet and psychologist as colleagues, and for that reason I have concentrated on it in this essay. Its usefulness, in the end, must depend on the view we take of literature, and I conclude by repeating a point made in the discussion of Auden's poem. If our view of literature is emotive – that it expresses or arouses emotion – then the theories it embodies are of no intrinsic importance, and it does not matter if they are true. Lyric poetry is clearly not a fruitful field for this use of psychology, since a lyric is nothing if it does not express an emotion, and perhaps it does nothing else. But if our view of literature is cognitive, if we like to praise Shakespeare or George Eliot for their wisdom, their insight, or their understanding of the human heart, then we can hardly refrain from comparing them with those whose job it is to study, more technically and rigorously – not the human heart exactly, but the human nervous system, the way human beings learn, and the endless fascination of human behaviour.

# Appendix I

## Undergraduate Courses in English Studies at British Universities

In most universities there is much discussion of teaching, examining and other arrangements. This is a time of quite rapid change, and intending students should keep in mind, when reading guides and prospectuses, the possibility of radical alterations.

### Entrance

Intending students must apply through the University Central Council for Admissions (UCCA), and should read the current issue of *How to Apply for Admission to a University*, available on application from UCCA, PO Box 28, Cheltenham, Gloucestershire.

Each university has its own entrance requirements, which the intending student must meet, but English departments may have additional requirements, or there may be special requirements for individual courses or combinations of courses. This information is fully available in an annual publication, *A Compendium of University Entrance Requirements for First Degree Courses in the UK* (London, Association of Commonwealth Universities).

### Degree choices

English, either literature or language, or American literature where it is offered and is thought to be closely related to English literature, may be studied in several kinds of degree programme.

(a) *Single Subject Honours B.A.* This is usually a three-year programme, except that at Belfast it is four years, and the Scottish honours M.A. is also four years. There is usually some requirement to read one or more subsidiary subjects.

(b) *Combined Subject Honours B.A.* The combination of English and another subject. With the above exceptions, this is also normally a three-year degree, but a number of universities require students who are reading for honours in a modern language other than English to spend a year in the country of that language. This means that the combination of English and French, for example, would involve four years' study. There may be some requirement to read one or more subsidiary subjects. Half the student's time is generally taken up with the study of English. The two halves of the course may be conducted independently of each other, leaving the student to make any connections, or there may be some requirement for truly joint work. The latter is not frequent.

(c) *Integrated Honours B.A.* Some universities, mostly newer ones, have tried to institutionalize the interrelation of study. For example, at Warwick English is studied in the School of Literature, and it is impossible to study it on its own. At Essex, too, discussion is under way to extend the study of literature to include joint degrees in literature and art, and to extend the work in Western European literatures, but not to establish a single subject degree. At Sussex, there are English courses in topics in history and literature, or philosophy and literature, taught jointly by a historian or philosopher and an English specialist; English literature is also read in such inter-disciplinary courses as the Modern European Mind, or Artist and Public.

(d) *General Degree B.A.* This is the kind of three-year programme (becoming steadily less common), which demands the study of perhaps five or more subjects, two or three of which are pursued further. English appears at all levels. Such degrees are sometimes given with honours.

Precise information about the organization of degree programmes involving English is set out by each university in its *Calendar* or *Prospectus*, and sometimes in a handbook which may be sent on request to a school or to an intending student. A list of such publications, and also publications issued by colleges which offer degree courses in English is the *Blue Book of Degree Course Prospectuses* published regularly by CRAC (see below). Schools or careers masters often hold files of such publications. A useful preliminary volume to consult is the annual *Guide to English Courses in the Universities*, 60p post free from the English Association, 29 Exhibition Road, London, S.W.7. This is a comparative guide arranged by university, and has an entry of two or three pages on each, setting out the kind of degrees available, any special entrance requirements, as well as listing details of the courses offered.

## Courses

A large proportion of the Single Honours degrees in English are degrees in English language and literature, and the English component of Combined Honours degrees also frequently involves English language study. Such Single Honours programmes allow the student to choose a strongly literary scheme of work, or a predominantly language one. Here, *language* generally means the historical study of English or related languages, such as Old Norse, Gothic or Middle Scots. The study of Anglo-Saxon (Old English) and Middle English, the two earliest historically defined periods of English is often a requirement, though this study is frequently based on reading the substantial literary texts in these languages rather than being philological or grammatical. A few programmes, such as that at Exeter, do not require language study after the first year, though they offer it to specialists. It is also true to say that medieval literary studies in English are firmly associated with such historical language study. Most programmes in language and literature allow only two alternatives – language or literature – with certain minimum requirements of both. Some, however, present a more flexible series of choices. At Leeds, for instance, there are certain local features combined with a choice of four programmes:

(a) is a predominantly literary course with a fairly strong element of philology;
(b) strongly emphasizes philology and medieval literature;
(c) is almost entirely literary, but requires some Middle English study (as well as, unusually, practical drama);
(d) is based on linguistics combined with medieval studies, *or* modern literatures, *or* Folk-Life Studies.

Combined Subject Honours degrees generally offer simply those parts of the particular Single Honours programme which would combine best with the other subject. The English language requirement is sometimes present in the English literature part of the programme, sometimes not. The intending student should consult the English Association's *Guide to English Courses* mentioned above for a succinct account under the headings of individual universities of the kinds of programmes offered in English studies, their language and literature requirements, and possible subject combinations.

It may be mentioned, however, that a confusion of terminology makes the use of such guides, as indeed of the publications of individual universities, difficult. The 'courses' are often given in the form of lists of the titles of examination papers which must be taken in the final B.A. examination. It is often the case that there are 'courses' or classes which correspond with each paper title, but sometimes not. The work is covered in a combination of other classes. Also, the titles of the papers may be relatively uninformative about the *nature* of the study. 'English literature 1360–1560', the title of an examination paper, could provoke study of many different kinds.

That said, however, we may turn to a brief discussion of the *kinds* of course. There are roughly two kinds of course, *historical* and *contextual*. In the first the reading is geared to the development of some kind of historical picture, of a writer, a form, or above all a period. In the second, the works to be read are placed in a context of different study, of ideas, of society, of other (perhaps contemporary or non-English) writing. We could think of these two kinds of course as intersecting vertical and horizontal paths. Obviously they are never mutually exclusive. At this point, the intending student is referred to a most useful publication which appears every other year. This is the *Degree Course Guide: English*, published by the Careers Research and Advisory Centre (CRAC), Bateman Street, Cambridge, 50p.

The current one for 1971–2 was published in 1971. A *Digest of Changes* appears in the intervening year. The CRAC *Guide* gives some discussion of the kind of courses offered at different institutions. These are most often historical surveys of the literature of particular periods. Clearly, since of its nature literature partly belongs to the 'past', of last year, last decade, or last century, there has been great pressure to make the historical picture the key one. Some university programmes seek to 'cover' the writing of the last four centuries, or perhaps further back. Some programmes abandon this 'coverage' to make room for the study of other associated or related disciplines. Historical discussion may be related to the notion of genres. Course titles such as 'The English Novel' or 'Naturalism in the Modern Novel' or 'Tragedy' may indicate this approach. Development in British university English courses has usually been in the direction of offering students options in addition to a central core of historical reading. Topics may sometimes be chosen for study in depth, which are partly historical and partly inter-disciplinary, such as 'Anglo-Saxon Art and Archaeology', 'American Studies including the film and plastic arts', or are chosen at will. There is also the question of 'criticism'. Sometimes this is itself approached historically, sometimes philosophically, and of course also practically and personally. The latter approach may be indicated by a course title such as 'Practical Criticism', but it must take place in any good reading, and is likely to be found anywhere in certain situations which cannot be signalled in a syllabus.

Each intending student will have his own preferences and interests which he may or may not seek to match with a degree programme. There are subjects which find a place in some syllabuses and not others. It is only possible to combine English with Arabic, for example, at Leeds and Manchester. Art, may be Art History or Fine Art, but at Exeter the English-Art combination requires practical work at the Exeter College of Art. Drama may be read as texts but sometimes may be run at such universities as Bristol, Exeter, Hull, Leeds, Manchester and one or two others associated with active university theatres by drama departments. Few universities find any place in their official English studies schemes of study for creative work, but Dundee does to a limited extent. American literature sometimes appears in options in course lists, but also sometimes as a part of an American Studies programme, which students in English may join to some extent. Commonwealth literature options are available at Edinburgh, Exeter, Kent, Leeds, Sussex and Swansea. It is impossible to give more than a brief hint of the possibilities here. There is no substitute for hard information available from one or other of the publications cited earlier.

The Open University started teaching in January 1971 by means of correspondence courses, local Study Centres and Summer Schools, backed up by radio and television programmes. English takes its place in the 'Inter-Disciplinary Foundation Course in the Humanities'. Students, at present they must be over 21, assemble 'credits' over a period of years to qualify for a B.A. or B.A. with honours. The credits must be made up from a combination of subjects. English is one. Information is available from Chris Batten, Admissions, The Open University, PO Box 48, Bletchley, Buckinghamshire.

# Appendix II

# Degree Courses in Institutions other than Universities

Because of the current situation of too many prospective students of English, and too few places to accommodate them in the universities, not all applicants for university places are successful. There are opportunities for studying for degrees in English at other institutions of higher education, such as some of the colleges of technology, polytechnics and others. These degrees include the University of London's external B.A. (External Registrar, Senate House, Malet Street, London W.C.1), or degrees authorized by the Council for National Academic Awards (CNAA) (3 Devonshire Street, London W1N 2BA). Further information about such courses, which cannot be dealt with in this book, may be obtained from the addresses given, or by consulting the following publications which appear regularly:

*Compendium of Degree Courses*, 1971 (CNAA, 1971).

*Compendium of Advanced Courses in Technical Colleges*: 1971–2 (Regional Advisory Councils, Tavistock House South, Tavistock Square, London W.C.1, 1971).

*The Directory of Further Education* (Cornmarket Press, 1970).

# Appendix III

# Postgraduate Studies in English in British Universities

## Entrance

Candidates are normally required to have a good honours degree, an upper second or better, in English or with English as a major component.

## Finance

The Department of Education and Science awards State Studentships for one year, or Major State Studentships usually for three years. There are many fewer awards than applicants, and while a first-class degree and a sound notion about the proposed work appear to be successful in gaining an award, not all students with upper second-class degrees are given money. The awards are related to specific intended work at a specific university. The Department publishes an annual pamphlet *Grants to Students 4: Humanities State Studentships and Major State Studentships* (1971).

The Association of Commonwealth Universities publishes a handbook of *United Kingdom Postgraduate Awards* tenable at British universities (1969–71 edition, 50p).

## Degree choices

The terminology at different universities varies. There are broadly five kinds of postgraduate degree or programme:
(a) A degree involving course-work, with or without a requirement to write a dissertation. This is normally a one-year programme, but in some universities it may require two years. It is usually an M.A., but may be a B.Phil., or an M.Litt. (Edinburgh). The programme may be made a requirement for candidates who hope to go on to a higher degree.

(b) A master's degree (usually an M.A.) awarded on the submission of a satisfactory dissertation.

(c) A research degree awarded on the submission of a dissertation which though original and a contribution to knowledge does not set out to have the scope and substance which would gain a doctorate. This is usually an M.Phil. or M.Litt. (at Oxford a B.Litt.).

(d) The Ph.D. or D.Phil. awarded on the submission of a substantial dissertation of unarguable originality and which makes a real contribution to learning in the field.

(e) Special programmes leading to Certificates or Diplomas for special vocations. For example, the Diploma in Applied English Linguistics at Leeds, designed for foreign teachers of English, or the Diploma in English as a Second Language offered at Bangor, for the same purpose.

Individual universities have different areas of specialization in English Studies. They may possess exceptionally good library or other collections in these specific fields, as Nottingham does in Byron, D. H. Lawrence and Tennyson. They may have vigorous groups interested in special topics, as Edinburgh and Lancaster have in linguistics. Further detailed information about matters of this kind may be obtained from the university prospectuses, or the handbooks which some departments and schools issue, or from:

*Graduate Studies, 1971*: volume 1, *Humanities* (Cornmarket Press, 1970), a directory of universities and subjects.

*Schedule of Post-Graduate Courses in the U.K.* (Committee of Vice-Chancellors, 7th edition, 1970).

There are several books on literary research. The most recent, which contains references to others, is George Watson, *The Literary Thesis: A Guide to Research* (Longmans, 1970), paperback.

# Bibliography

**D. J. Palmer,** *The Rise of English Studies* (Hull University Press, 1965). This readable history of the introduction of English into the British universities as a subject shows how a good number of the differences of principle in teaching and studying the subject arose by reason of its nature, and also from the time, in the last century, when it started to develop. This book is invaluable in putting some modern arguments in perspective.

**F. R. Leavis,** *Education and the University* (Chatto & Windus, 1948) and *English Literature in our Time and the University* (Chatto & Windus, 1969). These two books set out a powerful and homogeneous view of an ideal *rôle* for English studies in the university. It is obviously attractive to think of this view and an opposing view, but it seems impossible to do so clearly. It is always interesting to see a fight, and *The Times Literary Supplement* arranged one, with two opposing sides, by printing the following three pieces:

**F. R. Leavis,** ' "English" – Unrest and Continuity', a lecture published in *TLS*, no. 3509, 29 May 1969;

**F. R. Leavis,** ' "Literarism" versus "Scientism": The Misconception and the Menace', a lecture published in *TLS*, no. 3556, 23 April 1970; and

**Lord Annan,** 'The University and the Intellect: The Miasma and the Menace', a reply to the former piece, published in *TLS*, no. 3557, 30 April 1970. There is, however, no such simple opposition of single forces, as it is hoped the essays in the present book will show. It is quite possible to differ on good intellectual grounds from both Lord Annan and Dr Leavis.

**W. W. Robson,** *English as a University Subject: the F. R. Leavis Lecture 1965* (Cambridge University Press, 1965) is really confined to the Oxford and Cambridge English scene, and only parts of that, but has some interesting general points.

**Klaus Boehm** (ed.), *University Choice* (Penguin Books, 1966) has an essay on English Studies by Professor Brockbank, which now needs revision.

**David Daiches** (ed.), *The Idea of a New University* (Sussex) (André Deutsch, 1964), paperback, has a chapter by Professor Daiches on English Studies.

# Index

173

James VI of Scotland, 30–1
James, Henry, 128, 131, 135, 136, 137, 138, 154
Jespersen, Otto, 95
Johnson, Dr Samuel, 16, 31, 32, 34, 35, 39
   *Dictionary* (1755), 87
   *Lives of the Poets*, 24
   *Proposals for Printing the Dramatick Works of William Shakespeare* (1756), 30
Jonson, Ben, 27, 31, 32, 148, 157–8
*Journal of English and Germanic Philology*, 77, 122
Joyce, James, 61, 62, 64, 125, 126, 136
   *Finnegans Wake*, 51
Junius, Francis, 75, 76

Kent, University of, 166
Kafka, Franz, 153, 154
   *America*, 152–3
Keats, John, 56
Ker, W. P., 59, 61
Kolve, V. A., on medieval miracle plays, 70
Kott, Jan, *Shakespeare Our Contemporary*, 33, 48, 74
Kris, Ernst, 160
Kubie, Lawrence S., 160

Labov, William, 83
Laclos, P. A. F., *Les Liaisons Dangereuses*, 156
Laforgue, Jules, 49
Lancaster, University of, 170
Langland, William, 49, 59
Latin, writing and reading of in England, 58
Lawrence, D. H., 5, 125, 126, 170
Leavis, Dr F. R., 171
   *Education and the University*, 16
   *English Literature in Our Time and the University*, 2–3
   'English, Unrest and Continuity', 3–4
Leeds, University of, 165, 166, 170
   School of English, Commonwealth literature Programme, 107
Lesser, Simon O., 160
Lewis, C. S., 68
   *Studies in Words*, 57
lexicography, 86 ff.
limbo, 109
Lindisfarne, 85
*Linguistic Atlas of New England*, 81
linguistics, 65, 170
   and English grammar, 101
   general, controversies in, 96–7
   general, theory of and the study of the English language, 94
   historical and comparative, 77, 80
   theoretical, 101
   transformational-generative theory and English language studies, 101
literary criticism, history of, 12
   theory of, 12
literary history, 27 ff.
'literary quarrel, the' between England and America, 124–5
Locke, John, 148
   *Essay Concerning Human Understanding*, 154–6
London, 85
Lowell, Robert, 72
Lowes, John Livingstone, 18
Lucian, 61

McCarthy, Mary, 132
Machaut, Guillaume de, 49
Machiavelli, Niccolò, 67
Malamud, Bernard, 133
Mallarmé, Stéphane, 66
Manchester, University of, 166
Mann, Thomas, 126, 149
   *Dr Faustus*, 145–8
   *Lotte in Weimar*, 51
   *The Magic Mountain*, 54
Mansfield, Katherine, 103, 118
Markandya, Kamala, 116
Marx, Karl, 11, 19
*Meanjin*, 118
Mehta, Ved, 116
Melville, Herman, 128, 131, 137

Williams, William Carlos, 134
Wilson Knight, G., 33
Winchester, 85
Wittgenstein, L., 72, 95
Woolf, Virginia, 63–4

Wordsworth, William, 20, 49
  Lucy poems, 23
Wundt, W., 154

Yeats, W. B., 125
York, 85